VICTORIA WOOD COMEDY GENIUS

Her Life and Work

by her brother
Chris Foote Wood

D0533299

4005077

**Aberdeenshire
Library Service**

4005077

Askews & Holts	28-Aug-2017
792.702	£12.00

for Victoria

VICTORIA WOOD COMEDY GENIUS

Her Life and Work

by her brother
Chris Foote Wood
(Northern Writers www.writersinc.biz)

Cartoons by 'Rog' www.rogcartoons.co.uk
Cover design by Tom Gallagher

*Photographs of Victoria Wood in yellow shirt on outer front
and back covers are the property of Photoshot*

© Chris Foote Wood 2016

First published November 2016 by
The Memoir Club
12 Tower Road
Washington
NE37 2SH
0191 4192288
memoirclub@msn.com

All rights reserved. No part of this publication may be reproduced, stored in a retrieval system, or transmitted, in any form, or by any means, electronic, mechanical, photocopying, recording or otherwise, without the prior permission of the publisher and copyright holder, except for a reviewer who may quote brief passages in connection with a review for insertion in a newspaper, magazine, website, or broadcast. Chris Foote Wood hereby asserts his moral right to be identified as the author of this work.

British Library Cataloguing in Publication Data

A catalogue for this book is available from the British Library.

ISBN: 978-1-84104-596-2

Author Chris Foote Wood is donating all of his royalties from this book to charities associated with his sister Victoria.

Errors and omissions: every effort has been made to ensure that the contents of this book are accurate and true. Anyone wishing to make corrections, amendments, additions or deletions, please inform the publishers so that agreed changes can be incorporated in future editions.

Printed by JASPRINT, Washington, NE37 2SH

CONTENTS

INTRODUCTION

Victoria Wood was truly a 'national treasure', a phenomenon, a genius. My sister endeared herself to millions as a hugely successful stand-up comedienne and singer-songwriter, but Vic was so much more than that.

While voted the 'Queen of Comedy' and the 'best ever female comic' with her own unique style of comedy, Victoria also wrote and acted in her popular TV and stage plays. She showed her talent for drama as well as comedy, winning top awards for writing and performing the title role in her acclaimed TV wartime drama *Housewife, 49*. She was also outstanding as Eric Morecambe's mother in another TV film, *Eric and Ernie*.

Victoria was voted 'the person you would most like to live next door to', beating even the Queen Mother. *She was very annoyed,* said Vic.

Vic also wrote and acted in another TV film, *Pat and Margaret*, the story of two sisters reunited in a *Surprise, Surprise!* like television show after many years apart. One (Julie Walters) is a glamorous American TV star, the other (Victoria) a dowdy motorway service station waitress.

> ***My boyfriend had a sex manual but he was dyslexic. I was lying there and he was looking for my vinegar***

As well as sell-out performances of her stage show around the country, including the unique achievement for a solo artist of fifteen consecutive sell-out nights at the Royal Albert Hall (twice), Victoria wrote and performed in the TV sketch show series *Wood and Walters* and *Victoria Wood As Seen On* TV with her long-time friend and acting partner Walters and an informal cast of regulars including Celia Imrie, Duncan Preston, Susie Blake and Andrew Dunn.

A spin-off from *VWASOTV* was the spoof soap *Acorn Antiques*, loosely based on *Crossroads*. *Acorn Antiques* continues to this day as a stage musical, written by Victoria of course. In its first run at London's Theatre Royal, Julie and Victoria alternated in the lead role of cleaning lady Mrs Overall, just one of many characters Vic created that have found their way into the hearts of the British public.

" Looking for my Vinegar "

Quite a number of the sketches Vic wrote, including some she did not act in, have become particularly memorable. *Two Soups*, with Walters as the elderly, forgetful waitress, is still fondly remembered. It has achieved a similar status to the sketch *Four Candles* by *The Two Ronnies*, Barker and Corbett.

Another of Vic's memorable creations was the TV soap *dinnerladies*, set in a works canteen. Victoria is not the 'star', she is just one of a strong cast - it's what is called an 'ensemble' piece. Typically, Vic gave some of her best lines to others, and her fellow actors adored her for it - while complaining about Vic's frequent rewrites as she sought to make her scripts as good as possible.

Vic wrote and produced the stage musical *That Day We Sang* about a school choir reunion, later turned into a TV film starring Michael Ball and Imelda Staunton. And so Vic added producing and directing to her ever-lengthening list of talents. There is no doubt her unexpected death at the early age of sixty-two robbed us of many future delights.

Our great consolation is the legacy Victoria left us: forty years of hugely entertaining comedy, song and drama which we can still enjoy. I hope this book reminds you of your particular favourites, as well as telling you things you might not have known about my famous sister.

Chris Foote Wood
Darlington
November 2016

CHAPTER ONE

STAN AND NELLIE

Victoria Wood was the youngest of the four children of Stanley and Helen Wood (née Mape, known as Nellie). I was the eldest, thirteen years older than Victoria, with two other sisters in between. I and my first two sisters all have talent, but the joke was that Mum and Dad *kept trying until they got a really good one.*

While I missed much of Vic's childhood after going to university, I have had the joy and privilege of watching my kid sister develop her career over the years. I watched some of her very early performances and saw her years of struggle before she finally achieved her well-deserved national fame.

So where did Victoria Wood come from, and what was she like as a child? I have my own memories of course, and I also have a unique record in the Journal our father Stanley wrote almost every day for forty-four years and in which he recorded his life and that of his children, especially Victoria of course. Victoria's genius was very much her own, but we all inherit much of what we are from our parents.

Victoria was born at the Holyrood Nursing Home, Bury Old Road in Prestwich, north of Manchester on the 19th of May 1953. While I and my first two sisters were born in hospital, by the time Vic came along our parents could afford for Nellie to give birth in a private nursing home - hence Prestwich. After ten days, Mum returned with Vic to our family home in Bury,

In the Wood home, there was always music.

and it was in Bury that Victoria Wood was brought up and went to school.

It is tempting to think that Vic was named after another talented and famous stage performer, Matilda Alice Victoria

Wood, better known as the music hall star Marie Lloyd (1870-1922). As both our parents were ardent republicans, it's doubtful they were thinking of Queen Victoria.

Our Dad Stan kept three sets of diaries: a pocket diary, a desk diary and a thirteen volume Journal in which he recorded - often at great length - the daily 'doings' of him and his family. With a few gaps, I have inherited all three. They make fascinating if difficult reading: Stan's handwriting is not always easy to decipher.

Stan highlighted important entries in his Journal, such as the birth of his third daughter and fourth child:

May 19th 1953:

> *VICTORIA WOOD, 7lb 12oz, born at 8pm Holyrood Nursing Home, Prestwich - a lovely baby, beautiful in every way.*

Home for the Wood family in 1953 was a large, end-of-terrace house, 98 Tottington Road, Bury. It had a garage and an extensive rear garden that ran down to the Woodhill Brook, a small stream heavily polluted from dye works and paper mills. This large house was a step up from the nearby modest semi, 55 Ramsey Grove, our first proper home. After the war, with four of us at that stage, we 'lived in' with Stan's parents and two other family members in Chorlton-cum-Hardy, a pleasant Manchester suburb. In 1947 we moved the few miles north to Bury and two rented rooms at 104 Ainsworth Road. Mum cooked on a two-ring gas appliance - there were no other facilities apart from a shared bathroom. The rest of the house was occupied by our landlady Mrs Bagshaw and her numerous family. This was all standard stuff in the 1940s and early 50s.

Birtle Edge House, our family home from 1957, is an extensive, imposing building in its own grounds, high up on the edge of the Lancashire moors, overlooking a golf course and the Irwell Valley. It was built in 1908 as a holiday and convalescent home for 'poor boys' from Bury to enjoy fresh air and exercise away from their squalid living conditions and the soot and grime of the town. This mini-mansion suited the needs of our parents: it gave Stan peace and quiet to write his plays, scripts and music, and for the reclusive Nellie it was the haven from the world she craved.

Nellie did not like visitors and few made it up the long, winding, unmade track to our house.

Vic was a happy baby, with bright blue eyes and a mass of blonde curls. She was always smiling and gurgling happily: to my recollection she never had tantrums, and if she cried, she would be quickly and easily mollified. As a baby Vic never bothered with the crawling stage. She found her own unique method of propulsion - sitting on the floor on her bottom and propelling herself forward by pulling her legs in. Thus she scuttled around the house like a demented crab with great speed and enthusiasm.

Two things marked Vic out, even at just a few months old: a cheerful disposition which made everyone else happy, and doing things her own way. Vic recalled:

When I was very, very little I pulled faces a lot and made the family laugh.

Stan and Nellie met in 1937. She was just eighteen, he was twenty-five. When they married in July 1940, Nellie was five months pregnant with me: nothing unusual, especially during wartime. I arrived in December that year, Penelope was born in 1945, Rosalind in 1950 and Vic in 1953. Apparently, Nellie wanted to get each of her children off to school before she started with the next one. If so, Victoria must have been a 'mistake', but a happy one.

Our two parents were vastly different in character, temperament and in their own upbringing. Nevertheless, as so often happens, opposites attract. They fell in love at first meeting and had a lifelong, if sometimes stormy, marriage.

Where did Victoria's talent come from? From her parents, of course. It's my firm belief that Vic got her creative abilities mainly from Stan (although Nellie was herself much involved in the arts), and her drive and determination from her mother. One without the other, and there would have been no Victoria Wood, superstar. Both together produced one of the very brightest talents of our era.

Growing up, we children were very much aware of Stan's music, plays, stories and scripts. He played piano and had run his own dance band before the war. Writing under his pen name Ross Graham, Stanley Wood had his first novel published soon after WW2, he had great success with his radio plays, he had his stories read on the radio, and he wrote film, radio and TV scripts including a spell as a scriptwriter on *Coronation Street*. Vic's huge output was all her own, of course, especially her unique brand of comedy, but I believe that Stan pointed the way. Certainly he encouraged his hugely talented daughter and when she was still a teenager she helped him with some of his own projects including his well-received stage musical *Clogs!*

For all his obvious talent, Stan, an insurance underwriter, never gave up the 'day job'. Several times I urged him to do so, but he always said it was 'too risky'. Born in 1912, and having lived through the depression of the 1920s and 30s when a job meant the difference between 'getting by' and abject poverty, I can understand his decision. He had a wife and four children to support.

Stan and Nellie were determined that we four kids should have a far better start to life than they had had. They made sure we enjoyed a much better standard of living and, above all, that we had the best possible education. We all went to good schools, followed by university.

> *We'd like to apologise to viewers in the North, it must be awful for them.*   **TV continuity announcer**

In contrast to her laid-back and outgoing husband Stan, Nellie was a much darker and introverted character. She largely cut herself off from her working-class family and instead made friends in the Ladies Circle and the Costume Society.

As well and his musical and writing ability, Stan was a great organiser. In the years after WW2, he organised and ran a Christmas toy fair, taking over Bury's swanky Derby Hotel for a week. With toys difficult to get and very much in demand, these were hugely successful events with queues down the main staircase and out into the street. As an ex-navy man, Stan always knew where things could be found: he was a bit of an Arthur Daley. Stan also organised the annual Bury carnival, attracting top UK music and sports stars to do the official opening.

After the war, Stan qualified as an insurance underwriter. He was very good at it and became one of the top UK salesmen with the Manufacturers Life of Canada. At the same time, he continued to write stories, plays and scripts. He was particularly successful with his radio plays, several of which were broadcast on the BBC. It's interesting to note that some of the original *Coronation Street* cast such as Violet Carson (Ena Sharples) appeared in some of Stan's radio plays before the seminal TV soap started in 1960.

Stan himself wrote scripts for the *Street*, more I believe than just the one featured in Corriepedia, Episode 1237, broadcast in 1972. Stan wrote these wonderful lines:

> *Only one thing would worry me if I was Rita. Where could I get a hat to put on that hair? (Elsie Howard) Next thing you know, it'll be drugs - LSD and cannibals (Hilda Ogden).*

Victoria did a great skit of *Coronation Street* on TV. It is so authentic you might mistake it for the real thing! It's lovely to think there is this connection between Vic and her Dad. Stan wrote his successful stage musical *Clogs!* in 1975. Stan also wrote and produced sketches, songs and music for the big annual office 'do', and he played the occasional piano gig with a local dance band.

No wonder Vic said that when Dad was at home he was 'always writing'. He was. Stan did encourage his children, particularly with music. Disappointed with my all too obvious limited musical ability, he still found time to come and hear me play at dances when I joined a skiffle group. Naturally Stan was delighted when Vic showed her great musical talent early on. He got her to help with his band parts and bought her a baby grand piano.

In 1957 when Vic was just four and I was coming up seventeen we Woods moved from the urban surroundings of Tottington Road to Birtle Edge House, an extensive single-storey building, a sort of mini-mansion, out in the countryside. It was, and is, a huge house, very isolated, on the edge of the moors overlooking Walmersley golf course and the Irwell Valley. Used in WW2 as an air raid defence centre, Birtle Edge is an imposing building in three acres of grounds.

The house had no mains water and was not connected to the sewage system; the electric and telephone connections were dodgy, and the access road unmade, rough and narrow, but to Stan and Nellie it was their dream home. For the reclusive Nellie, it was an escape from the world. As Vic said, we never had any visitors. That suited Nellie fine.

For all of us there was ample room to spread our wings. We four children each had a substantial bedroom of his/her own. Nellie had her sewing room and Stan his dressing room and study. For a family in which each one of us was able to do our own thing, it was ideal, at least for three of us four children.

I and my first two sisters found lots to do and we belonged to all sorts of clubs and other groups. My interests included various after-school clubs (railway, stamp and chess) as well as competing for the school cross-country and athletic teams. I was also active in the YMCA, Bury & Radcliffe Athletic Club, pantomime, choir and two youth clubs. I was even a Sunday school teacher for a while. Penelope and Rosalind were also occupied with their own interests.

For Vic though, spending much of her time in her own room, it was a lonely existence. Much of it I didn't see at first hand. In 1959, when I was eighteen coming up nineteen and Vic was six, I went to Durham University, King's College Newcastle, to study civil engineering. After that I got married, had three children, and settled in Bishop Auckland in County Durham.

While Nellie, for her own unspoken and unexplained reasons, 'didn't want to know' about me and my three children, Stan was a caring father and grandfather. He often telephoned to ask how we were all doing, and he was only too pleased to tell me about the exploits of his three daughters. In fact, he praised them more to me (and in his Journal of course) than he did to them! Stan also brought my three sisters to Bishop Auckland to see my family, and they were all very much taken with their nephew and nieces.

Life was planned by a committee while the clever ones had popped out to the lav.

It wasn't until Vic herself went to Birmingham University in 1971 that she reconnected with me on a more regular one-to-one basis. She invited me down and I was very happy to go a few times. She was already performing whenever and wherever she could, including at folk clubs and on the local radio. She hooked up professionally with folk singer/comedian Jasper Carrott and was 'support' on one of his early tours. It was great for me to see their show at Newcastle City Hall after

19

she left uni.

That was the first time that I had seen my sister perform in public. It was a largely student audience, and they gave Vic a hard time. Here was this plump young woman - no glamour-puss, she - singing her low-key, bitter-sweet songs while accompanying herself on the piano. She looked so lonely, young and vulnerable; I wondered if she would survive. But she did, and how!

When there were quips from the audience, she answered them back in no uncertain manner. She carried on with her set, putting her songs across with verve and bite. Eventually, the audience quietened down and just sat and listened to her clever lyrics and jaunty piano playing. At the end, they gave her great applause. I was so proud of her!

After that, it was a case of following Vic's burgeoning career with pride and joy. My second wife Frances and I (we married in 1977) went to as many of Vic's shows as we could. Vic would leave us tickets at the box office, and she always made us very welcome to see her in her dressing room after the show. It has been a pleasure and a privilege to see Vic develop her career so masterfully and in so many different ways: I will always be grateful for the happenstance that made me the brother of such a talented individual.

Frances and I first met Vic's husband Geoffrey Durham when they did their two-person *Funny Turns* show at the Sunderland Empire. Despite Vic's success on TV with *New Faces* and *That's Life*, I estimate there were no more than forty people in the audience. There were so few, that when Geoff (as mock Spanish magician The Great Soprendo) asked for someone to lend him their wedding ring, there were no takers.

Gallantly, I offered my wedding ring. I didn't want the show to grind to a halt! But Geoff refused to take it. Always the consummate professional, he realised in an instant that if it leaked out that he had taken something for one of his tricks from his brother-in-law, the press would have a field day. He finally got one from someone else in the audience, made it disappear and (of course) brought it back again in some unlikely place.

When a close relative marries, you hope against hope that you will be able to get on with their new partner. With Geoff, there were no problems whatsoever. As far as I could see, Geoff was the perfect husband for my intense, hugely talented sister Victoria. He was kind, caring, considerate, even-tempered and wholly supportive of his wife personally and professionally. Likewise, she was equally caring of him. To me, the two of them were perfectly matched.

When their two children came along, Grace and Henry, with Vic and Geoff they seemed to constitute the perfect family. You only need to be with a family a short time to sense any tensions there might be, but I never felt anything like that with Vic, Geoff and their children.

Frances and I visited them at their homes in Silverdale near Morecambe, and in London's Highgate, as well as at their secluded holiday home near Skipton in North Yorkshire. The two children always seemed happy, content and secure - no tantrums when we were there. Vic and her two kids were particularly close. At our regular annual family gatherings around Christmas and New Year, we would play games. Vic, Grace and Henry made such a formidable team, they would always win - so much so that I had to split them up to give someone else a chance.

Our Dad Stan died in 1993, and it was Geoff who took charge of the funeral arrangements. When my mother Nellie declared she didn't want me at the funeral, Geoff - for all he loved her - took my part. He insisted that, not only was I going to be at the funeral, I would help carry the coffin and I would read a poem during the non-religious service. I am forever in his debt for what Geoff did for me that day.

I'm all for killing animals and turning them into shoes and handbags. I just don't want to have to eat them.

It was a terrible shock when Vic and Geoff separated and then divorced. She went for therapy, while at the same time writing some of her best work. Geoff moved just around the corner, no more than 100 yards away. Although divorced, he continued to be a close and caring father to his two children with almost daily contact.

Even more remarkably, when Vic became ill with the cancer that ultimately killed her, Geoff was regularly at her side, along with Grace, Henry and Vic's closest sister Rosalind who had also settled in London some years before. It speaks volumes for Geoff's continuing affection for his ex-wife - and for her continuing regard for him - that he rendered this final service for her.

Again, it is a measure of Geoff's humanity and character that he has remained a good friend to me, despite the divorce. When two people you love divorce, you want to stay friends with both. Very often that is not possible and you are forced to 'take sides'. Not so with Vic and Geoff.

When I decided late in life to take to the stage professionally with my own (very modest) one-man show, Geoff gave me all the advice and support he could. Geoff himself toured with his own one-man show very successfully for many years. I saw it often. Now Geoff no longer performs, he is - amongst other things - a professional producer, yet he gave me the benefit of his experience and knowledge free. With his advice, my show has done well at the Edinburgh Festival Fringe for the past three years.

Did Vic and I have disagreements? Yes we did, but what brother and sister don't argue? I mention a couple of such occasions in later chapters. But for balance, I would like to mention the one occasion when Vic actually congratulated me - about a joke I told(!)

Some comics are always 'on duty', cracking jokes at every opportunity. Others reserve their joke telling for their professional performances. Victoria was very much one of the latter. When she was on stage she was the nation's number one female comic, if not the nation's number one comic, as I hold she was - never mind Billy Connolly! With her public, Vic would joke and quip as only she can. But at home, she was 'just Mum', concerned with domestic matters and her children's welfare and education.

In private, Vic was her own individual self. She very definitely did not tell jokes at the dinner table - but I did! No, I don't class myself as being anything like as funny or as clever as Vic in any way, shape or form, but I do have my moments. It was at the family home in Highgate that this unusual and remarkable event occurred. Now remember, in our family, praise is hardly ever given. Here's the joke.

George Brown, Foreign Minister in Harold Wilson's Labour government, liked a drink, and he had an eye for a pretty girl. At a diplomatic reception in Brazil, George had had too much to drink (as usual) when he spotted a tall, slim girl in a full-length, red sheath dress. As the band struck up, George sidled up to her and asked her if she would like to dance.

This lovely creature turned to George and said: 'No Sir, I will not dance with you, for three reasons. First, you are drunk. Second, this is not a waltz or a tango, it is our national anthem. And third, I am the Cardinal Archbishop of São Paulo'. 'That's very good,' said Vic, 'the perfect example of a three-part joke'. Wow! My multi-award winning sister, who had entertained millions on stage and on the TV screen, was actually praising me. Mind that was the only time. Mostly my jokes and stories were received with polite laughter. But let's be thankful for small mercies.

> *She's really, really tall and really, really wide. If she had a suitcase on her head she'd look like a fitted wardrobe.*
> **Kimberley's friend**

'I fear being my mother' - that's what Victoria told Chrissy Iley of *The Daily Telegraph* in 2012. On another occasion Vic said she had become a replica of her mother with her short temper. Now why would my hugely talented and successful sister Victoria say those things? Whatever your theories on nature versus nurture, there's no doubt that we inherit much of ourselves, our physical characteristics, our brain power and our talents, from our parents - both of them. And surely our upbringing, schooling and childhood experiences must also play a significant part in what kind of adults we become.

So let's start with our parents, Mum and Dad. Who exactly were they, and what did we four children - and Victoria in particular - inherit from them? Both Stan and Nellie came from humble beginnings. Stan's father and mother both worked for the Post Office, although his doting mother Eleanor had 'ideas above her station' after being brought up in a household with servants. They prospered sufficiently to be able to move from Moss Side in central Manchester to a nice little semi in Chorlton.

Stanley Wood was an only child, while Nellie Mape came from a big family with six children, not counting two who died young. The Mapes existed just above the breadline: the father John, a labourer, was unable to work due to wounds sustained as a soldier in the First World War. Mother Ada, a cotton spinner, was the sole breadwinner until her children were old enough to go to work.

As Vic had a troubled relationship with mother (as I did also) I'll start with her. Mother, known to her family as Nellie, was born Helen Colleen Mape in 1919, the second oldest surviving child born to Ada and John Mape in highly industrialised East Manchester. Her middle name Colleen should give you a clue: this was an Irish Catholic family whose grandparents had emigrated from Ireland around 1850 due to the potato famine.

The Mapes were poor, dirt poor. There was never enough to eat. Nellie wrote that she went hungry every day. At lunchtimes she and other kids would go around the local factories and beg scraps from the workmen.

Nellie went to three or four Sunday Schools. Not that she was religious - she was later a committed atheist - she had worked

25

out that by getting the minimum number of attendances at each, she could qualify for the much-prized annual Sunday school tea at each of them. Now I know why, when we were little, Mum would say 'if you're still hungry after your tea, fill up with bread and jam. No-one leaves the table hungry' (as she had often done).

As soon as they reached their fourteenth birthdays, Nellie and her elder sister Nora had to leave school and go to work. It was an economic necessity. Nellie went to work as a progress chaser in the nearby steelworks, run by the English Steel Corporation. Now Nellie was very, very bright, and everyone knew it. In her final year at school, aged thirteen, she was put in charge of the 'dunces'. Nellie taught them by telling them stories.

There was no question of Nellie staying on at school beyond the minimum leaving age of fourteen, but she made up for it later in life. Aged forty-nine, when her third child Rosalind went to Loughborough Art College, Helen started her own degree course at Manchester University. She got a BA and an MA and became a lecturer in English Literature at Bolton Tech.

As a girl, Nellie would put on little plays for the local kids on the street corner, making up stories which she acted out with another girl. Nellie was also 'boss of the street', dictating what games were to be played, who was to be in each team and so on. She took charge of the weekend expeditions to nearby Philips Park: mothers would happily allow their young children to make the trip if they knew that Nellie Mape would be in charge.

Nellie was a rebel at school. She argued with the teachers: unheard of in her day. In her final year, Nellie's form teacher sent her to the headmistress with a note recommending her to be head girl. The head teacher threw it back at Nellie: 'Tell Miss O to send someone else'.

In her scrappy bits of memoir, Nellie recounts how an early teacher was explaining the word 'fat'. She lifted little Nellie up onto her desk: 'this is a fat girl' she said. Even in her final year, when the teachers at her Catholic girls school wanted a message taking to the boys school across the road, they would say: 'Send Nellie Mape, at least the boys won't whistle at her'. What all this did to Nellie's self-confidence, you can only guess.

But all that changed when Nellie went to work, aged fourteen and a day. As the only girl in a factory with some 2,000 men, she suddenly became an object of interest, and indeed, desire. Her job involved going all around the works, so the men and boys would get plenty of opportunities to see her, and for her to see them. Nellie had lots and lots of boyfriends, and I mean lots.

It was all very innocent in those days, no sex involved. There might be kissing and cuddling in the cinema or on a park bench, but nothing more. Nellie loved going out, to the cinema, theatre or dance hall. She liked to go hiking, and she made the most of her opportunities. If a boyfriend turned up two minutes late, he would be dismissed and a replacement found very quickly.

Now I know exactly how many boyfriends Nellie had, and I mean exactly, because she wrote them all down. At just turned eighteen, Nellie met the tall, blond, handsome piano player Stanley Wood aged twenty-five, and that was it. Stan was boyfriend number 106 - I kid you not! 106 boyfriends in four years is on average one a fortnight. Good going, Mum.

As well as getting through boyfriends at a rate of knots, Nellie had two other passions she followed relentlessly. She and Nora were both keen members of the Independent Order of Rechabites, a national temperance and welfare organisation with over a million members. Aged sixteen, Nellie took charge of the local junior branch in Manchester. At the same age she won the Rechabites annual essay-writing competition: prize one pound.

But Nellie had upset the all-male hierarchy of the Rechabites by calling them 'old fossils who should get up to date'. On being presented with her award she was told that she had won it, not so much because of her own efforts, but thanks to the 'excellent teaching' she had received from her Rechabite tutors. Nellie was very proud of her achievement and in a rare intimate moment, she showed me her essay in a bound volume of the Rechabite magazine.

Nellie applied herself equally passionately to politics. She joined the Young Communist League and at elections canvassed for both Communist and Labour Party candidates.

She was particularly committed to campaigning against the rise of Fascism: she demonstrated in support of the Republicans during the Spanish civil war. She supported the 'Free India' movement.

At seventeen or eighteen, this led to a clash with her father. He did not hold with women being involved in politics, and as an old soldier he was all for King and Country. One dark and stormy night Nellie came home after a street demonstration, cold and sopping wet. She took off her hat, coat and shoes and sat by the fire as her sisters made her a cup of tea. Her Dad, who persistently suffered from a wound that would never heal, got himself into a paddy.

'You'll stop all this political nonsense, or leave this house!' he demanded. 'Very well, I'll leave tomorrow' replied a defiant Nellie. 'No you won't, you'll leave tonight' declared her now furious father who literally threw her out of the house into the rain and dark, bolting the front door. Nellie's sisters ran upstairs and threw down her hat, coat and shoes. Nellie never went back, but was (I believe) reconciled with her father when I was born. She took me, his first grandchild, to see him in hospital where he died shortly afterwards.

Vic recalled her mother in an interview with Richard E Grant. She said:

We had a house full of junk, but also full of books, up and down all the walls, all the partitions were shelved, so we had to walk everywhere sideways. She (mother) read obsessively and so did I. If my mother didn't like anything, all she said was 'Tch, tch,' that's a very Lancashire thing, 'Tch, tch'. She didn't discourage me.

Of her Dad, Vic said:

> *My father encouraged me because he was a frustrated performer, he was an insurance man and he wished he wasn't an insurance man.*

Stanley Wood was a completely different kettle of fish. For a start, he was an only child, born in 1912. And, rather than being brought up in the slums of East Manchester, Stan was raised in a semi in the leafy suburb of Chorlton-cum-Hardy. His Dad, our Grandfather John Wood, had been a sergeant in WW1. John was at the Dardanelles and also fought on the Western Front, where he won the Croix de Guerre. Typically, he never spoke of it and we didn't find out about his medal until after his death.

John Wood was tall, athletic, a good swimmer and a first-class crown green bowls player. He was the strong, silent type, 'one of nature's gentlemen' who spent all his working life in the Post Office, rising from telegraph boy to chief telegraphist at the GPO's Manchester office. But it was Stan's doting mother Eleanor who had much the greater influence on our artistic father.

Symptoms of pregnancy: moody, big bosoms, irritable. I've obviously been pregnant for twenty years.

In two words, Stan was spoilt rotten by his indulgent Mum. To her, he was the 'golden boy' who could do no wrong. Eleanor passed on to Stan her love of the theatre - she had performed on stage as an amateur - and she encouraged him in his piano playing and play-writing. Stan went to Chorlton High School, but had to leave at sixteen due to lack of finance. His first job was at a flour mill.

Even at that young age, Stan showed his talent for writing and producing (apart from singing and playing the piano, he was never much of a stage performer) and also making some extra cash. Each year the Chorlton Old Boys Theatre Group put on a show of one-act plays and sketches, for which the headmaster paid the author £1. Stan quickly twigged that by writing five different items, each under a different pen name, he could get £5 instead of a solitary quid!

The enterprising Stan played piano to accompany silent films in the local cinemas: he played piano in a 'big band' and he also ran his own dance band. For some extraordinary reason Stan called his band the *Blue Hoodlums*. His supportive mother Eleanor even had a telephone installed to take bookings, but how she reacted when asked 'is that the *Blue Hoodlums*?' I have no idea. My 'posh Nana' (as I called her) later in life still had the bottle to get bookings for me in my brief career as a solo folk singer in the late 1950s!

In the 1930s Stan tried his hand at journalism, writing for motorcycle and car magazines. He also got a job as an insurance claims inspector, returning to insurance as his main occupation after WW2. Stan signed on as an ordinary seaman with the Royal Navy, but to please his mother he later took the exams and became an officer.

Unlike his Dad, Stan was no war hero. His idea was to keep as far away from the fighting as possible. He was cagey about what he did in the war, during which he wrote his first novel *Death on a Smokeboat, a story of Espionage at Sea*. It's a most authentic tale, and led us to believe he might have been involved in the secret service, something that would have suited his talents admirably. We just don't know.

But something we do know he did that was also right up Stan's street, was as a musician and theatre producer. He did his basic training on HMS *Royal Arthur*, a land-based establishment which had been Billy Butlin's first holiday camp at Skegness and was taken over by the War Office for the duration. Stan played piano in the officers' mess, a good way of getting out of the more boring jobs and earning some extra cash. As a naval lieutenant based in Plymouth, Stan came into his own by putting on theatre shows for the lads on leave.

The main theatre in Plymouth would be hired by the week and Stan would put a show together. His shows were very popular and raised lots of money for war bonds. He was also keeping up morale. Stan had no difficulty in finding musicians, comics, jugglers and acrobats, but his main task was to get together a chorus line of dancing girls. After weeks or months at sea, that's what the lads most wanted to see!

Stan would trawl the local pubs (and he did like a drink) for the necessary talent, and when he saw a pretty barmaid, he would ask her if she wanted to take part in one of his shows. A tall, blond naval officer with the gift of the gab - how could any girl refuse?

'What will I have to do?' the girls would ask. Stan would demonstrate a few rudimentary steps: de-doo-dedi-doo, de-doo-dedi-dah, and they would sign up. What Stan didn't tell them, was how skimpy the costumes were!

Stan also raised morale among the matelots when he was made editor of the navy magazine *Guzz*. Previously rather a staid publication, Stan enlivened it with jokes, cartoons - and pin-ups. He wrote to all the major film studios in the UK and America asking for pictures of their female stars, Betty Grable and so forth, and the studios were only too glad to oblige.

One story Stan recounted was that of a grizzled old CPO (chief petty officer) a long-serving navy man and a bit of a stick in the mud. For a laugh, some young sailors placed the *Guzz* equivalent of a centrefold in front of the old man, saying 'what do you think of that?' It was a photo of a buxom young woman, naked but with her vital bits hidden by two coils of a thick mooring rope.

The old man studied the picture for several minutes. He leaned back in his chair, sucked his pipe, took off his glasses, cleaned them, put them back on and studied the photo again, but still said nothing. Finally he spoke. 'I've got it! No doubt about it, that's definitely four inch hemp!'

> *Foreplay - you don't have to. We can always do it afterwards, if there's time.*

Stan continued to write throughout his life. After *Smoke Boat* he wrote several more novels, 'about six' he told me, but some he failed to finish and no more were published. He was much more successful with radio, writing documentaries, stories read by Wilfred Pickles, and plays which were not only well received but also paid well. He wrote for *Northern Drift* and *Talkabout* and was an early scriptwriter on the seminal TV soap *Coronation Street* which started in 1960.

Corrie was also a good earner for Stan. 'When I'm short of cash, I just give Les Duxbury [producer] a ring' he told me, getting another 13 episode stint. Stan also wrote a successful musical stage play *Clogs!* which premiered at the Duke's Playhouse, Lancaster, and was performed at other northern theatres but didn't make it to the West End.

In one respect at least Stan and Nellie were totally united: they were determined that all four of us children should be given a much better standard of living than they had had as children, and above all the best possible education. Stan was always doing extra jobs. At one time he would hire himself out to drive a local family to Blackpool for a day at the seaside. He would sit in a local pub and write as they enjoyed themselves, before bringing them back that night. Nellie also worked: she was a telephonist in Manchester and later conducted opinion polls and surveys.

I had so many detentions, my parents thought I was on the nightshift.

When she was in her forties, Nellie went to night classes to catch up on her schooling. She passed her GCE 'O' Levels and 'A' Levels and gained entry to Manchester University as a mature student in 1966. There she won a BA and MA, going on to become a lecturer in English Literature at Bolton Tech. Nellie Mape had finally made it - what a marvellous achievement!

So why did Vic say she feared becoming her mother? It was Nellie's obsessive hoarding: it got worse as she got older. In 2011 Vic told Chrissy Iley of *The Telegraph*: 'I'm an anti-hoarder. I fear being my mother because she hoarded'. Iley: 'That's very controlled'. Vic: 'There's no harm in a bit of control. My mother was terrible. She'd get things off mail order, bedding, towels and shoes. I mean, she was in bed, she didn't even walk. No idea why she was ordering shoes. Thank God she didn't have the internet. She liked parcels in the post'. Iley: 'Maybe that was her version of eating?' Vic: 'She did eating as well. She had a food problem and a hoarding problem'.

Vic always kept a tidy home. She also conquered her 'food problem'. But more of that later. Stan and Nellie went to see Victoria perform whenever they could. Stan often praised Vic in his Journal, although he could also be critical.

Stan wrote in his Journal: 3rd November 1986 Monday:

> *This day Victoria on the cover of the Radio Times, baggy suit, bare feet a jolly clownish pose, very nice, but smile looked a bit forced. As if she had to be posed several times.*

10th November 1986 9.30:

> *Victoria Wood was very good - excellent - but* Acorn Antiques *had gone slack & non-claustrophobic. V looks marvellous.*

Stan's last mention of Vic in his Journal: 5th March 1987 Thursday. A newspaper headline:

> *Victoria, Queen of Comedy.*

Stan died in 1994, Nellie seven years later, both aged eighty-one.

Nellie in particular always hoped her children would be famous one day. In Victoria, she got her wish - many times over. Although she often gave her husband a tongue-lashing, Nellie's love and affection for Stan never wavered. One November 13th, she wrote in her diary:

> *Anniversary of Wood's death. I remember what I promised him when I first saw him dead on the pillow - that I would be brave as he would expect, and 'good' - not to cause trouble for the children etc. Today I am calm, counting my blessings, past and present, and wearing my bright orange shirt, to please his memory. He likes red best but I haven't*

got a red shirt - yet!

Just like the Infant Mozart

CHAPTER TWO

JUST LIKE THE INFANT MOZART

One night, Stan and Nellie noticed a light under Victoria's bedroom door. She was just six years old, a quiet girl who didn't cause any trouble. Intrigued, the two parents crept to the door and peered through the crack. Six-year old Victoria was studying the *News Chronicle Song Book*, which had the words and music of popular songs of the day. Victoria had got hold of blank music sheets, of which her musician father had a great number, and she was copying the music from one to the other, note for note, as Stan noted in his daily Journal.

After that, Stan gave Victoria the job of copying his band parts, paying her a penny a bar - quite good pay for a young girl. He bought a baby grand piano which was located in the main entrance hall, for Victoria to practice. Her facility at the keyboard stood her in good stead in later years when she was performing on stage. It is quite a skill to be able to play, sing, make jokes and hold an audience all at the same time, and Victoria had it in spades.

Well, that's the way Stan used to tell it. When he first told me, Vic was seven. Then she was six, then five. So I took an average. On re-reading the daily Journal Stan wrote up almost every day for forty-four years, 1943 to 1987, I find his original written account a little more prosaic. But at least we know that Victoria was seven when Stan knew for certain that - at last - he had produced a child with real musical talent.

This is what Stan wrote in his Journal: 18th December 1960, Sunday:

This morning I found Vicki in her pyjamas in the playroom with curtains drawn from last night and no great light, engaged at the News Chronicle Song Book, *reading every word and note bar by bar. Rather like the infant Mozart.*

Stan did pay Victoria a penny a bar to transcribe his music (three staves - two thirds of a penny for two staves), but in reality that came much later. Rather than six or seven years old, Vic was in fact in her teens when Stan gave her that job. Vic was also still in her teens when Stan started writing the music and lyrics of songs for his stage musical *Clogs!* for which he engaged the help of his hugely talented daughter. But that was Stan - he was a story teller, and while his stories were invariably based on fact, he would often 'gild the lily'. Why let the facts stand in the way of a good story?

All three of us elder children, myself and sisters Penelope (known as 'Penel') and Rosalind had piano lessons and could play reasonably well, but none of us had Vic's musical ability and creativity. For us three, music was just a part of our busy lives. For Vic, shy and unhappy, music was her main outlet from a very early age.

Victoria also showed an early talent for drawing, with her first artwork. Still aged three, this drawing of Mum and Dad is remarkably mature:

20th January 1957 Sunday:

This brilliant cartoon (and noticeable likeness) was drawn by Victoria Wood, unaided, at the age of three years and eight months.

Victoria's first day at school. Stan wrote: 13th April 1958

Tomorrow Victoria Wood goes to school for the first time (bless her huge heart).

15th April 1958:

Vicki loves school. She has three boyfriends, and is in a quandary as to which one to marry.

Then there was a glimpse of Vic's unique way of looking at the world. Stan wrote: 18th November 1959

Vicki [six] said the school dentist looked inside her mouth 'with a knife and fork'.

I don't think you could get the pill in Bury. You were lucky if you could get yoghurt.

And then came the first glimpse of Victoria's musical gifts. Naturally Stan was delighted when Vic showed her great musical talent early on. Vic's great strengths included the ability to grasp a full story while remembering all the detail. In December 1960 Stan wrote:

Vicki (seven yrs seven months) told me the whole story of 'Bal Krishna' [Hindu story]. She has a remarkable grasp. She chanted through lots of people getting through different presents.

Victoria's first joke! Stan records this exchange with his youngest: 19th August 1961

Me (explaining): 'D'Artagnan was one of the Three Musketeers'. Vicki [aged eight]: 'I suppose he was deaf' (must-get-ears).

When Victoria was still only eight, she had an epiphany when she saw Joyce Grenfell's one-woman show in Buxton. 'It was the first time I'd seen anyone stand on their own on stage,' she recalled. 'I didn't realise that there were jobs like that before - that one could stand on stage and speak, with no props except for a nice frock and people would die laughing.'

14th April 1962: this is the day that Victoria (just before her ninth birthday) says was the day when she realised for the first time that a woman could go on stage and command and entertain an audience with only a piano for accompaniment. The way Vic told me, she was left behind when her two elder sisters, Penny and Rosalind, went backstage to see Grenfell after the show. On being told there was a third sister, Grenfell insisted on coming out to meet her and did so, making a huge impression on the shy Victoria.

As Vic told it, she was six at the time, but in fact she was almost nine - but no matter, we all recall things differently. Either way, this was truly a turning point in Vic's life. Dad made a brief note, 14th April 1962 Saturday:

We are now devoted slaves of Joyce Grenfell. Lovely time in Buxton last night. Later Penelope and Rosalind went in her dressing room. (Vicki felt I had let her down and complained bitterly to her mother - in getting lost backstage and being scared of stagehands).

12th May 1963:

Vicki [coming up ten] composed Tune No. 5 and marked it Ralentando.

Victoria did well in junior school and was generally top of her class. That all changed when, aged eleven, she went to Bury Grammar School Girls. Like many youngsters then and now, she found it hard going among girls who seemed all to be at least as clever as she was. Her school work suffered, and Vic admitted to doing as little as possible.

As her musician father Stan recognised very early on, Victoria had great musical talent. Like him, she became a fine piano player, and she also played second cornet in the Bury Town Band. This latter ability she used to advantage in a sketch she wrote, a skit on the film *Brassed Off*. In the sketch a local brass band are looking for a lead cornet player. The band members are sceptical when a young blonde woman (Vic) arrives to audition for the position. They are astounded when Vic plays a brilliant solo. 'You played great love, but you still can't join the band', she is told. 'Ok, fair enough', says Vic, and off she goes. Now there's a twist!

Smashing birthday card made by Vic for Dad: 1st July 1963 [Stan's 41st birthday] Vic's own card.

> *She refused comics saying 'I have to finish something first'. Card says 'I'm not too old to have birthday presents', and has pop-up window inside. 'When you are old and grey, we'll still not forget your birthday. To Papa from Victoria'.*

Stan noted, 27th March 1968:

Band Jokes: Vicky [fourteen] to lad she secretly likes: 'You look like a werewolf' 'You don't have to worry, I won't be biting you'. Son to father (who play 1st & 2nd cornet) 'Do you like my tie, Dad?' 'Tie? Ah thowt it wer tha tongue hanging out'.

I've got a degree; does that mean I have to spend my life with intellectuals? I've also got a life-saving certificate, but I don't spend my evenings diving for a rubber brick with my pyjamas on.

Victoria characterised her childhood as being solitary and unhappy. Our mother Nellie suffered from depression, had eating problems and didn't welcome visitors. Neither Vic nor I can remember anybody coming to our house other than the postman, meter readers, workmen etc. It was Nellie who wanted to be alone. Easy-going Stan didn't mind. He had a study where he could write in peace and quiet. Vic spent most of her time at home in her room with her books, her piano and a television. For evening meals at Birtle Edge House, Stan would usually be away working - he would often meet clients in the evening - and Nellie would never sit with us children. Mum would cook meals in the kitchen and serve them through a hatch. I left home to go to uni in 1959. I was eighteen, Vic was six. After that, I rely on her account that family evening meals ceased and Vic would take food into her room. She was supposed to make herself packed lunches for school, but never did.

Aged eight or nine, only one child came to Vic's birthday party, despite Dad's effort to recruit others. And there was no indication at junior school of Vic's future career. She said she once narrated the nativity play but didn't take part. But she was junior school biscuit table monitor.

Vic made few friends at Bury Grammar School Girls. In November 1989 she went to a reunion at Crimble's Restaurant near Rochdale with fifty-five former pupils. At times Vic said she had no friends at school, or one, or two. Perhaps others remember differently. But there was music. At twelve, Vic joined the Bury Orchestra and Bury Military Band. She also played in the school orchestra.

On the *Wogan* TV show, Gloria Hunniford asked Vic about her school reunion, twenty-five years after leaving. 'I had a horrible time at school,' said Vic, 'I was always being sent out and made to stand in the corridor'. At the reunion Vic said she was looking for 'love bite' Beverley. 'I was really jealous of her at school. She was really cool and never went to swimming. She was always on her period'.

Vic told Richard E Grant: 'I'm not nostalgic for my childhood, really, at all. Because I didn't really enjoy it that much. It was quite boring, and I was quite miserable a lot of the time'. Vic later wrote: 'I've been writing songs since I was about fifteen. I wrote an end-of-term show at my school, I just remember one song from it which was a commercial for Cupid's Kiss corn-plasters:

> *With a Cupid's Kiss corn-plaster, You'll have feet like alabaster, Be a Mrs, not a Miss, With a Cupid's Kiss. 'I never said it was funny. I only said I remembered it.'*

Throughout her childhood and schooldays Vic was reading, reading, reading - as I did at her age. Vic 'stole' books from Bury Library, but in 1999 she sent the Council £100 and a letter of apology. Vic also confessed she kept £13 she had raised from a charity sponsored walk.

One book she liked was *Modern Masters of Wit and Laughter* by Anthony Armstrong and others (1938). Vic highlighted another book as having a big influence on her. That was a novel, *The Swish of the Curtain* by Pamela Brown (1941). Seven children convert an abandoned chapel into a theatre where they can perform their own plays. Dame Maggie Smith said:

I wanted to act before I read this book, and afterwards there was no stopping me.

Vic liked to read a particular passage from the end of the book. The kids have formed their own theatre company and have won a prestigious award, the Seymore Trophy:

In a dream Lyn walked up to the floodlights, her cheeks flushed to match the red velvet of her dress. 'Are you the little producer?' she was asked by the amazed Mrs Seymore. 'Well, yes in name,' she replied, smiling up into the friendly eyes, 'but the play produced itself'. She took the heavy statue and turned to the applauding audience. What was she expected to do now? Why, of course - behave just as in the word-picture she had painted to the others that day at Browcliffe. She curtsied, then looking up to the familiar faces in the gallery, she kissed her hand. The applause grew deafening, and gradually the people rose in their seats, still clapping. The theatre stood and cheered and stamped, while Lyn bowed and smiled for an eternity.

After reading this favourite passage, Vic would look up with a beaming smile. 'Now, wasn't that good? That's what I wanted to do,' she would say. I can't remember Vic curtseying for anyone, not even the Queen, but she certainly fulfilled this particular childhood dream - and how!

When I told jokes about cystitis, people would write in and say, 'I've got cystitis and it isn't funny,' so I would reply, 'Well, send it back and ask for one that is.'

Vic's other great consolation was playing the piano. There was always a piano in the house - Stan would practice from time to time - and doting Dad bought Vic her own piano for her 15th birthday

I played anything, anything I could read. I was very good at sight-reading, she said.

But Stan took her to the theatre, and in July 1969 Vic went with the school to Stratford.

Stan made sure we all got the chance to hear good music.

16th February 1963:

Went to Free Trade Hall with Victoria, Penelope & Justin [?] for Leonard Bernstein and the New York Philharmonic Orchestra. Rossini, Schubert, West Side Story dances, Tchaikovsky's A flat Minor No. 4 Symphony. Wonderful experience. 105 musicians, of which 70 were strings. A superb sound.

In his obituary of Victoria, the *Guardian*'s Stuart Jeffries said that Vic found few friends at Bury Grammar School Girls, quoting her previous comments:

I wasn't completely unpopular ... but I didn't feel I was in the mainstream with people who were really having a wonderful time ... I'd look at other girls and wish I could be

like them, interested in boys, meeting in the Wimpy bar on Saturday mornings and going to discos. I was also addicted to sugar, which makes you depressed.

she added:

So I think I was always slightly depressed as a child and a teenager.

According to her own account, Vic did not make friends at school. At one time she said she had no friends, another time she said just two. But when she went to a reunion at BGS Girls, she enjoyed it very much. In 2012 she told Chrissy Iley of *The Telegraph*:

I've been to a school reunion. It was brilliant. I was the last to leave. I was there all day with my friend and that was twenty years ago.

Iley: 'Maybe they all came to see you? Vic: 'No, I don't think they did. They came to see the school and the teachers. I was no big deal, honestly'. Iley: 'I can't imagine that was the case. Did you keep up with the people with whom you were reunited?' Vic: 'No. I've had the same two friends. I just see them. Two friends from school, that is. I do have more than two friends'.

Vic also made it clear she neglected her school work. After being top of the class in her junior school, she found it hard to adjust among a class of girls who were all as clever as she was. Bury Grammar School Girls - like the adjoining BGS Boys school I attended - was and is an independent, fee-paying grammar school with a first class academic record. I was clever enough (thank you, Mum & Dad!) to get a free scholarship to the Boys school. Stan was delighted when Lancashire County

Education Committee agreed to pay Vic's school fees, but Victoria's initial school reports were not good.

7th February 1965:

> *Went to Vicky's Parents' Evening. Much queuing up. Music teacher asked if she was lazy. All said she was sloppy & untidy.*

Vic says she didn't do her homework, she copied off other girls and did as little work as possible. Because of the lack of homework (according to Vic) she was not allowed to take part in a school play until she was seventeen when she played Autolycus ('a rogue') in Shakespeare's *The Winter's Tale*. I still have the programme. The school magazine described her Autolycus as 'hilariously roguish'.

Vic also got a music credit for the production, along with her school friend Lesley Schatzberger. Years later, Schatzberger set up the charity Jessie's Fund which helps disabled children to communicate by using music. Vic became a patron, saying:

> *I was delighted to become a Patron of Jessie's Fund because its mission seems to me abundantly clear: that music is there for everybody, it helps everybody, no matter what their physical limitations or their difficulties with vision, hearing, or communication.*

Vic's school reports started to improve, but she still had mood swings. Stan wrote, 8th January 1970:

> *V very silent and morose.*

15th January 1970 Thursday:

> *A week of musical improvement - Vicky jolly and cheerful, Ma doing excellent essays on Ben Johnson & the Jacobins,*

me actually working and making prospects. Last night, in fear and dread, we went to the Grammar School Parents' Evening, expecting a night of misery and remorse, of humiliation and abuse, but loved it all & had most optimistic chats with V's teachers. All agree she has Something.

17th March 1970:

Tuesday. V very glum & morose. Suffering from diet, end of term (fed up with school) no letter from Bob, Miss Lester told her off for wearing duffle coat at school, called it 'deliberate defiance'. Tonight she went to Octagon, Pinter's Caretaker *not very good.*

23rd March 1970 Monday:

V has cheered up, telly having been mended.

Success belongs to other people - like imitation fur fabric pencil cases.

There are two points in Victoria's life that she firmly identified as turning points and essential to the ultimate development of her career. One was seeing Joyce Grenfell on stage at Buxton, The fact that Grenfell took the trouble to come out and see her afterwards also made a huge impression on young Vic: as a performer herself she always, always met her fans at the stage door afterwards no matter how tired she was.

The other turning point was the Rochdale Youth Theatre Workshop. 'Thank Heaven for Rochdale Council' Vic would say. How she got there is one of those wonderful things that happen due to serendipity - pure chance, her sister Rosalind going to school in Rochdale. I went to Bury Grammar School Boys, and Penelope and Victoria to BGS Girls. For some reason - I've never enquired why - Rosalind went to a Catholic school in Rochdale, six miles away. Rosalind got involved in the Rochdale Youth Theatre, took her younger sister Vic along, and the rest, as they say, is history.

For the fifteen year old Vic, she found to her delight that for the first time she could be involved in something that she really wanted to do, something that suited her personality and her inclinations. She could get up on stage, act a part and be appreciated for it. More than that, she found she was best suited to comedy roles and was even more appreciated. And further, she discovered she could write things that other people could act out on stage. After years of isolation in her bedroom, it was heaven!

But you can't help noticing that, at the same time that Victoria was experiencing the first flowering of her acting and writing talent, she also acquired her first 'real' boyfriend Bob Mason. They wrote and performed sketches together. Bob Mason had won the *Daily Mirror* young poets competition. They collaborated on a sketch show that Vic wrote and performed at Buckley Hall Youth Detention Centre, rated a success.

Our parents rarely praised us: we were just expected to do well and being top of the class was taken for granted, par for the course. Stan was careful not to lavish praise on any of his children: Nellie never would. Vic thought this was a northern trait. In 2009 she told the *Mail*'s Frances Hardy: 'If they like you in the North of England they won't say, 'You were wonderful, darling!' They'll say, 'You weren't bad' or 'I didn't mind it''. Vic told *The Telegraph*'s Chrissy Iley: 'My father was more of a praiser, not hugely more, but I knew he liked what I did because he was very interested in songwriting and comedy'.

In a 2011 interview with *The Telegraph*'s Chrissy Iley, Vic was asked if she thought one is born funny?

> *I think you are, but having a funny parent helps the way you develop. My father could be funny. My mother had no sense of humour, as she was always claiming, as if it was something to be proud of.*

She says this with a sudden flash of barb. Her mother must have inspired a whole mixture of interesting emotions.

> *My mother, she didn't believe in praise. She'd never say anything was great. I think that's quite northern, to not make people feel too good. I didn't mind if she was proud of me or not, it didn't bother me. I was never trying to please her.*

As Victoria was going through her teenage years, she could not help but notice that her Dad Stan was having some success with his own writings. Stan would always tell us about his latest production.

20th April 1966 Wednesday:

> *BBC suggest* The Court Marshall *[play] be extended to sixty minutes! Hurray!*

Stan had a particularly bruising encounter with the BBC over his latest radio play before it was finally broadcast. It may well be that, seeing Dad suffering as he saw his work being 'butchered', that Vic became determined to be in control of her own creations: 10th December 1966 Saturday:

> *Up at 6am, caught 7.20 to London. In Langham Studios by 10.30am. Producer told me they had cut off a big chunk & rewritten the end. It ran 1 hr 10 min. It had also been*

ruthlessly subedited. I really suffered a good deal - all this butchery and came away feeling, if not actually carved up, at least black & blue. Left at 1.30, caught the train & was back in Manchester for 4.20. Fabulous. In 10 hours I had been to London & back, put in 3 hours at a BBC rehearsal & eaten two meals. Ronald Mason [producer] was pale & had dark shadows under his eyes. His woman-Friday was magnificent. So was June Tobin [actress].

17th December 1966 *Radio Times*:

Afternoon Theatre Call Corporal Watson by Stanley Wood, with Ronald Herdman, Allan McClelland and Walter Fitzgerald. I think the play had a very high listening figure. There has been a great & widespread reaction among friends and acquaintances. Great stuff!

I wasn't unpopular, just not needed by anybody.

Victoria also had her run-ins with the BBC. She resented and utterly rejected the official who tried to tell her what was funny, and she was left fuming when the Beeb demoted her 2009 Christmas Special *Victoria Wood's Midlife Christmas* from the prime-time slot she had been promised. Months later, Vic told *The Guardian's* Decca Aitkenhead that the BBC executive who had made the decision didn't even bother to tell her, and passed her in the corridor without speaking.

I just think it's rude, said Vic, *I treat them with manners, I turn up on time and I make my shows on time and I make them as well as I can. I want there to be mutual respect, and there isn't any.*

In 1988 Victoria wrote to BBC2 controller Alan Yentob and told him in no uncertain terms that she felt no-one at the BBC cared about her work. In 2016 *The Mail on Sunday* Arts correspondent Chris Hastings quoted her letter:

> *Nobody has ever bothered about what other work I'm doing, or taken any notice of me while I was there or acknowledged any awards that may have come the way of the programme.*

Yentob promised her 'great care and commitment', but Victoria told him:

> *I've met the LWT chaps from Audience With and they all seem perfectly decent and professional, I can't really think of a way of getting out of it.*

Vic did the *Audience With* programme, broadcast on December 10th 1988. It was a huge hit and gained two BAFTAS.

In 1994, Yentob, by then controller of BBC1, commissioned Victoria's TV film *Pat and Margaret* despite opposition from some of his own executives. Again it was a great success, with over ten million viewers.

> **There was all the worry of making sure you had left the house with clean underwear, as well as fretting about pronouncing Chekhov.**

Stan often took Victoria to the theatre. On this occasion he was 'name checked' from the stage by the star comedian, actor and radio presenter Wilfred Pickles, for whom Stan had written stories and jokes.

23rd March 1968 Saturday:

> *Excellent trip with Vicky to Richmond [Yorks] to see Gaslight by Patrick Hamilton at the Georgian Theatre, with Wilfred*

Pickles & co. He announced us from the stage 'Friends from Bury'. We went backstage & had a chat for 3 or 4 minutes. Mabel [Pickles' wife: 'Mabel at the table'] was very nice - quiet, gracious and queenly. Wilf was very friendly. V said nothing.

22nd March 1969 Saturday:

Very pleased with Northern Drift *at 9.30pm. They had* The Best Boy *[by Stan]. Not at all bad. Still plodding on with* Clogs! *[Stan was writing a stage musical based on Lancashire life].*

1st October 1969:

V to Stratford.

3rd January 1970:

I have done a clean-up version of Ma in the Middle *& will send to Pat Sandys of Yorkshire and/or Granada [TV]. On Monday I will phone Peter Eckersley [later to play a crucial role in Victoria's story], a cod title Bean Jest.*

6th January 1970:

Am revising Clogs! *for shorter and simpler version for Ian Watson of the Century [Theatre].*

21st July 1971 Wednesday:

The happy day, most encouraging letter from Marion Head, television agent, about 'Lorraine' and James B of Granada liking it. Had I been asked to write for Coronation Street *etc? She would also handle my Radio Plays.*

18th September 1971 Saturday:

Have finished first rough draft of Gallipoli. V is doing music for me.

Victoria was doing her drama degree at Birmingham University 1971-74. *Clogs!* took so long to get off the ground, even with Vic's help, that it was 1975 before Stan's musical drama was first performed on stage.

4th January 1975:

> To Duke's Playhouse, Lancaster, having booked a single ticket. 'The third of the three Lancashire plays will be a brand new musical *Clogs!* by Stanley Wood. The Duke's Playhouse has not as yet performed a new musical and we are greatly looking forward to the challenge, and with such a well-written and entertaining story this should prove to be a great hit'.

20th March 1975 The Stage:

> A New Musical by Stanley Wood, set in a Lancashire Village at the turn of the century and called *Clogs!* is to be premiered at the Duke's Playhouse, Lancaster in repertoire presentation that opens on March 27.

By this time Victoria had appeared on TV in *New Faces*, but it would be 1978 before she made her big breakthrough with her own musical stage play *Talent*. But she was making progress. She sang her songs on local TV in a four part series *St John On...* 'St John Howell takes a light hearted look at life with songs on Home, Money, Food and fashion'. Producer Edmund Marshall was impressed with Vic's two minutes ten seconds.

She also performed on the local folk programme *Springs to Mind* and on the BBC's *Camera and the Song*.

SISTERS, SISTERS!

1 Three sisters (l-r) Penelope, Victoria and Rosalind (c.1968)

2 Happy together (l-r) Victoria, Rosalind and Penelope

3 Chris hugs his beloved Nana Wood

4 Sgt John Wood won the Croix de Guerre in WW1

5 Lt Stanley Wood in his WW2 naval uniform

6 Nana Wood (Eleanor Brigham) loved the theatre and was herself a stage performer

ERNEST G. LOCKETT & STAN WOOD

—Present—

THE BLUE HOODLUMS DANCE BAND

★ ★ ★ ★

OUR NAME. Recently, short stories about the misadventures of a village dance band have appeared in a well-known musical magazine. The author called it the Blue Hoodlums Band chiefly because this name was sufficiently outrageous to be a satire on some of the weird and wonderful titles used by many bands to-day. The author, content to leave it at that, was happily writing stories in his rat-infested garret when a knock came at the door and in walked a bloke who played the saxophone.

7 Stan advertises his band in typically jokey fashion

8 Stan (left) with two of the Blue Hoodlums

9 Wedding Day July 11th 1940, Manchester Register Office. Nellie was five months pregnant with their first child Chris, conceived when the pair made up after a huge row

10 The Woods, back row (l-r) Stan, Nellie, Grandad John Wood; front (l-r) Great-Gran Mrs Brigham (Eleanor's mother), Chris, Nana Eleanor Wood (holding tight her precious first grandchild)

11 The Wood family's penultimate home, 98 Tottington Road, Bury, Lancashire (recent picture)

12 Tottington Road, back garden (top) c. 1955

*13 Tottington Road,
back garden (bottom)*

14 Stan's first car, an Austin Seven Ruby, Penelope at the wheel c. 1958

15 Family portrait late 1953: Chris at the back,
(l-r) Nellie (with a rare smile), Victoria, Rosalind, Penelope and Stan

16 Grim faced Nellie with baby Victoria

17 Happy Stan bounces baby
Victoria on his knee

18 Picnic in the park: Chris took this shot with his Brownie 127

19 Three sisters: Penelope (left) and Rosalind hug their baby sister Victoria

20 As a toddler, golden-haired Victoria was always happy and smiling

21 Little Victoria loved to plodge

22 Cheeky Victoria at five years of age

DEAR FATHER I KNOW YOU WILL JUNE 1960 LIKE MY LETTER SO THATS WHY I AM SENDING IT TO LOVE FROM VICKY DADDY X X X X X X

23 Letter to father from his loving seven-year-old daughter Victoria

24 Family caravan holiday: Stan and Nellie relax near Ben Nevis 1957

10.0 ——449.1 m.——

Belle Chrystall in
**'THE STORY OF
SYLVIA MORRIS'**
A radio biography of the Lancashire girl who became famous in the theatres of Europe as Zoraita
Written by Ross Graham *(Stanley Wood)*

Narrator	Philip Cunningham
Sylvia Morris	Belle Chrystall
Marion	Rosalie Williams
Jack Leith	Harry Hewitt
Madame Barletta	Violet Marquesita
Mr. Culling	Ian Catford
Mr. Ashworth	Fred Fairclough
Henri	Arthur Lawrence

With Charles Gardiner, Heinz Lederer, and Doris Speed
Music arranged and directed by Jack Hardy
with Ada Alsop and Violet Carson
Produced by Norman Swallow

25 Under his pen name Ross Graham, Stan had great success with his radio plays. Violet Carson and Doris Speed later became stalwarts of Coronation Street, *Stan also writing scripts for the long-running TV soap*

26 Birtle Edge House was often cut off in winter. Stan and Nellie clear the snow c. 1980

27 'Darby and Joan': Stan and Nellie c. 1990

All photographs in this section are the property of the Author

Of BOHEMIA

POLIXENES, King of Bohemia - - - Sylvia Sherwood

FLORIZEL, Prince of Bohemia - - - Judith Slater

ARCHIDAMUS, a lord - - - - - - Judith Holt

OLD SHEPHERD - - - - - - - Christine Hurley

CLOWN, his son - - - - - - Judith Lyne

AUTOLYCUS, a rogue - - - - - Victoria Wood

SERVANT - - - - - - - - Hazel Page

MOPSA ⎫
     ⎬ Shepherdesses - - - ⎰ Belinda Haworth
DORCAS ⎭
                                ⎱ Janet Heron

COUNTRYMEN: Margaret Bateson, Katherine Brackenridge, Cathie Brown, Evelyn Douglas, Leonie Himelfield, Noelle Hoolahan, Judith Holt, Lynne Shaw, Jennifer Sheldon, Jane Wadsworth.

COUNTRYWOMEN: Hilary Beswick, Phillipa Buckley, Hilary Chapman, Gillian Holiday, Louise Shearer.

MUSICIANS - - - Marjorie Beswick, Joy Mendelsohn
                                          Diane Randle.
Sylvia Brierley, Lesley Fitton, Elaine Harling, Sally Nuttall, Lesley Schatzberger, Louise Shearer.

TIME AS CHORUS: - - - - - Margaret Bateson

Scene: Sicilia and Bohemia.

MUSIC composed by Jane Belfield, Lesley Fitton, Elaine Harling, Joy Mendelsohn, Sally Nuttall, Lesley Schatzberger, Victoria Wood.

Costumes, scenery and properties have been made by members of the school.

There will be one interval of twenty minutes during which refreshments may be bought, and our exhibition visited.

Programme page, showing Victoria (16) as actor and musician in her school play, Shakespeare's The Winter's Tale, *December 1969*

CHAPTER THREE

LET'S DO IT!

Let's Do It, Let's Do It, Do It Till Our Hearts Go Boom. Go native, creative, living in the living room. This folly is jolly; Bend me over backwards on me hostess trolley! Let's do it, let's do it tonight!

For all her relentless determination to succeed in her chosen career, Victoria still hankered after love, marriage and children: well, not so much marriage (although she eventually did marry) but certainly love and children. Not only did she manage all three - as well as reaching several pinnacles of success in the entertainment business - Vic has my huge admiration and respect for giving her two children, Grace and Henry, as 'normal' a childhood as possible. Along with her husband Geoffrey Durham - who continued to be a close and caring father even after their divorce - Vic made sure her two kids were sheltered from intrusive media interest.

There was no chance of Grace and Henry becoming 'showbiz kids'. Hardly any photographs of the two children have appeared in the press: two exceptions were when Vic was awarded the OBE and then the CBE. Eight-year old Henry made a brief appearance in Vic's 2010 BBC Christmas Special. Grace gained backstage experience working on the *Acorn Antiques* musical. Both parents made space in their busy professional lives to spend quality time with their children.

Be mighty. Be flighty. Come and melt the buttons on my flameproof nightie!

At first Vic and Geoff were intent on bringing up their family in the peace and tranquillity of Silverdale, a lovely village on the far side of Morecambe Bay. But as both of them had to spend a lot of time in London due to their work, they made the decision to move to the capital as the best solution all round. They settled in their spacious Georgian house in Highgate.

I once asked Vic how the children were getting on at junior school in Highgate, considering they were the offspring of rich and famous parents.

That's not a problem, said Vic, *all the other parents are millionaires too.*

Remarkably, the house provided a good deal of privacy despite being very close to the centre of Highgate. Vic told *The Mail*'s Frances Hardy:

It was our way of having an ordinary life. In London it's easy not to be the focus of attention, especially when Sting lives in the house just behind you.

Not bleakly, not meekly, beat me on the bottom with a Woman's Weekly. Let's do it, let's do it tonight.

Thanks to Mum and Dad, both youngsters have grown up to be well-grounded, likeable adults. It's no surprise that both are musically talented. Grace Durham is now a well-established, up-and-coming opera singer (mezzo-soprano) who has sung at Glyndebourne and indeed all over the world, and has gained a number of prestigious international awards. Henry Durham is a musician who now concentrates on writing and has formed his own company.

As a teenager, Vic had to put up with unwanted sexual advances. One time in the cinema, a man started stroking her leg during the film. She was too nervous to tell him to stop. 'Lucky it wasn't a double feature', she quipped. Maybe that was why she used to wear leg-warmers under her trousers. In October 1969 Vic told *The Times* she was accosted in the street by a man who asked her to perform an obscene act.

Describing life before her first boyfriend Bob Mason came along, Vic said:

> **All my friends started getting boyfriends. But I didn't want a boyfriend, I wanted a thirteen colour biro.**

Writer and comedian Viv Groskop described Vic's famous quip as 'the most true thing ever written of teenhood'. Vic said she looked upon the 'fast' girls who were the first to have boyfriends almost as if they were another species. She couldn't understand 'why they bothered'.

Victoria did eventually venture into the dangerous world of 'boys'. She admits to having two early encounters. In a 1990 TV interview with Clive James, Vic said:

> *I didn't have a proper boyfriend until I was fifteen. I had a date about two years before, but it was not what I would call a serious relationship. He was called Vince. He wore a teddy coat. He put his hand down the front of my dress in the pictures. Then there was Brett.*

Vic's one and only 'proper boyfriend' was Bob Mason, who she met at the Rochdale Theatre Workshop. Getting involved in the Theatre Workshop was in many ways the making of Victoria Wood. For the first time in her life she found she could do things - acting and writing - which were appreciated by other people. This occurred by one of those incredible coincidences that are pure serendipity.

I went to Bury Grammar School Boys and two of my three sisters, Penelope and Victoria, went to the adjoining but separate Bury Grammar School Girls. Our middle sister Rosalind instead went to a Catholic School in Rochdale. With ten years between me and Rosalind and thirteen years to Victoria, our Dad would refer to his two youngest as 'the little ones'.

Back to the boyfriend. Although Bob dumped Vic for another girl when they went to different universities, he had helped to bring Vic on as a writer and performer, and we must all be grateful to him for that.

Biographer Bruce Dessau says of Vic:

> *Years later, she would look on the summer of 1968 [aged fifteen] at the Workshop as the happiest time of her life. First and foremost there was the acting, the writing and all the organisational things that must be done to put on a theatrical production. But Bob came a close second. They were an 'item': they went everywhere together and did everything together.* Well, maybe not sex.

Stan wrote in his Journal: 31st January 1970:

> *Vicky goes out with Bob Mason. V said: 'We're going to get married, you know, when I'm twenty-three'. She is going to meet his parents.*

6th December 1970:

> *We had been talking about Bob & V grunting to one another - he says nothing romantic etc.*

7th September 1971:

> *V & Bob are going to decorate the den. They are much together, and observed through windows and in the garden, V shrieking as she rides on B's shoulder down side path In other words, much canoodling, snogging, or spooning.*

Bob Mason was a local lad who had won a national poetry competition. They started writing songs and sketches together. When Vic went to Birmingham University in 1981 she expected that their relationship would continue. Bob, also studying drama, went to university in London, met 'another woman', and fell in love with her. Vic got the old heave-ho. She didn't look for anyone else, but concentrated on building a career as an entertainer - no easy task.

Victoria told Clive James:

> *I had a proper boyfriend for four years until I was twenty. Then he told me he had fallen in love with this girl. I was inserting triangles into his jeans to make them into flares, so I carried on and sent them to him in a parcel. I thought he would be so touched and mortified that he would come back to me. Months later he sent me a postcard saying 'got parcel, jeans v poor'. He couldn't even be bothered to write the word very.*

On another occasion, Vic said:

> *that when she was 'dumped', she was even more determined to succeed in her career to make him regret it. 'I hope he's suffering' she said, with her usual laugh to indicate she didn't really mean it. She also said that Bob had left her with a host of uncompleted songs. She didn't throw them away, but added words and music as required: 'Waste not, want not'.*

> *I had this boyfriend. He wrote the words. I wrote the music, it was all very cosy and romantic, then he found someone else. I was left with a load of tunes and no lyrics - I should be grateful to that girl.*

I thought you could get pregnant if you swam backstroke in the same lane as a boy who'd just swum the butterfly.

But when love, true love, came to Victoria Wood, it came in a flash (and that's not a pun!). Geoffrey Durham was a former librarian from Surrey turned actor and magician. Vic met him when she got the job as MD (musical director) for a show in which Geoff was appearing in the lead role as Buffalo Bill. Jude Kelly, now a producer, said:

> *In 1975, after graduation, I took a job at the Leicester Phoenix, working with Alan Rickman, among others. Here, I persuaded the management to offer Victoria a job as musical director and pianist for some of the shows. One was Dracula in which I played Mina Harker [Minnehaha?] and the lead was taken by an actor called Geoffrey Durham.*
>
> *Not long after I introduced them in the Green Room, she let me know Geoff and she had become an item. It was exciting: they made each other laugh so much - they 'got' each other. Victoria had had some relationships before but never a boyfriend in that way, and it introduced me to another side of my friend. The one that wanted family, children (and) who had a subversive sense of humour but didn't want to live an outlandish Bohemian life. She was never materialistic, but she did like nice things, cosy things.*

I can certainly confirm that, when she was not working Vic revelled in domesticity. Her relaxation was to be a wife and mother at home with husband and children - later mother with children and ex-husband living around the corner - just doing the ordinary things. In many ways it was a complete contrast with her experience as a child growing up, with her parents and her siblings all doing our own, different, things either in our own separate rooms, or out of the house.

The result has been the closest relationship I have ever seen between a mother and her children. As a father who eventually became estranged from his children, Vic's achievement is something I can only admire.

So, with Victoria and Geoffrey, it was very definitely love at first sight. In many ways, Vic and Geoff were made for each other. They had an easy relationship that I have rarely seen in other couples. Visiting them at home in Silverdale or Highgate, or in their holiday home near Skipton in the North Riding of Yorkshire, there was never the slightest sign of any tension between them. They always seemed to me like a younger version of 'Darby and Joan', as affectionate and contented a couple as I have ever met.

For Vic, Geoff provided something that she had craved for but never found before: a loving partner who supported her in every way. Having someone 'in your corner' to give you the praise and support that every entertainer wants, but also to give advice and helpful suggestions when needed, was a huge boost to Vic's confidence. No longer did she have to plough a lone furrow.

Wikipedia says:

> Geoff encouraged Vic to develop a stand-up routine, punctuating songs with comedy.

Geoffrey was born in East Molesley on July 22nd 1949, making him four years older than Victoria. They met in July 1976 at The Phoenix Theatre, Leicester, where both were in the musical *Gunslinger*. Alan Rickman was Chief Blackmoon, Geoffrey was Buffalo Bill and Vic was both MD and piano

65

player Wilhelmina Fifty Fingers. 'He had a wig, fake tan and a suede jacket' recalled Vic.

Geoff taught Vic some magic tricks. In 1977 Geoff, as the Great Soprendo, played the Silver Jubilee Victorian Music Hall on Morecambe's Central Pier, put on by the Duke's Theatre of Lancaster three times a week, June 20th to September 3rd. Vic and Geoff decided to stay in Morecambe and rented a first-floor flat, 12 Oxford Street, overlooking the bus station, at £13 a week. They were there for four years.

At the time that was the only work they had between them. As things improved, they moved to a better flat overlooking the sea, and then to their own home in Silverdale (with orchard) across Morecambe Bay. When Vic and Geoff first became a couple living in a Morecambe flat, Mum Nellie was a bit worried and sent Stan to check up on them. As Stan told it, he went up the fire escape and found the back door unlocked. It was early on a Saturday morning, and he crept inside to find two figures fast asleep on the floor in two separate sleeping bags.

Eventually one stirred. 'Are you alright, love?' said one. 'I'm alright, are you alright?' came the reply. 'Yes, I'm alright' was the rejoinder, and with that, both went back to sleep. Without announcing his presence, Stan crept out. He reported back to Nellie that there was nothing to worry about:

they're just like an old married couple, he said.

Geoff very successfully developed his stage persona as 'The Great Soprendo', a fake Spanish magician. He appeared as Soprendo in the touring show he and Vic did together for several years, *Funny Turns*. He played the first half and she the second. It was as a magician (and a very good one indeed) that Geoff later toured for a number of years with his own one-man show. Geoff also appeared on the children's show *Crackerjack* and Channel 4's *Countdown*. He's also been a stage and film actor. No longer performing, Geoff is now a creative consultant in TV, theatre and film.

I thought Coq au Vin was love in a lorry.

Touring with Vic, Geoff took some of the pressure off her by dealing with practical matters such as management, and making sure the theatre piano was properly tuned. Being married to Vic didn't result in Geoff giving up his own career: far from it. When Geoff stopped performing in 2008 he had made 700 TV appearances, and had done 7,000 shows on five continents. He went out with a bang, topping the bill in the Magic Circle Christmas Show of 2008. In January 1990 he dropped his Great Soprendo persona and became simply Geoffrey Durham, conjurer.

Geoff also provided spiritual comfort to his very driven wife. Geoff has been an active Quaker since 1994 and has written two books on Quakerism. He introduced Vic to the Quakers: I'm sure it fitted in with her general philosophy of tolerance and concern for others. Wiki quotes Vic:

> As I've got older, I am more interested in having a belief. If you don't it makes everything seem pointless. To only think 'you're alive, you have acne and then you die'.

It took four years for Geoff to persuade Vic to marry him. Eventually they did marry, in 1980. It was going to be on February 29th but Morecambe register office didn't do weddings, only issuing funeral certificates, so they had to switch to Lancaster register office and Saturday March 1st.

To say their marriage was a quiet affair is an understatement. In a 1990 interview with Clive James, Vic revealed

> that she and Geoff were married in Lancaster at 9.30 in the morning. By 9.50 we were having spaghetti on toast. I had been doing a show, and my clothes had been stolen from my car the night before. I was still in costume for the wedding: we had pictures taken (of the wedding) but Geoffrey left them on the bus.

There were no rings, and no family present. Victoria did not tell her parents she and Geoff were getting married, but at least she sent them a postcard nearly two weeks after the event. Stan could not hide his disappointment (he had also missed my marriage to my first wife Helena, due to us eloping to Scotland when we were students).

13th March 1980:

> Vicky married, PC from her (postmarked) Thurs 10th March 1980. A dreadful day.

Vic and Geoff toured together with their stage show *Funny Turns* which opened at the Duchess Theatre on May 12th 1982. Vic also had a solo show *Lucky Bag* which had a five-week run at the King's Head, Islington starting October 1983.

'Control freak' or just highly organised, Vic made sure the children she wanted came along at just the right time to fit in with her career. She wanted to conceive at the start of the year to avoid clashing with her touring, so she flew back to London from Dublin to be with Geoffrey. Grace was born with the help of an epidural and synchronised swimming on the TV in the 'Fergie suite' at the prestigious Portland Hospital, two months after the Duchess of York Sarah Ferguson had gave birth there. Vic told *Woman* magazine:

> that she had found 'a couple of long ginger hairs' under the pillow.

Grace's middle name Eleanor comes from her paternal Grandmother, Dad's mother and my posh Nana, Eleanor Wood. Vic and Geoff's second child Henry William Durham also born at the Portland.

Vic used childbirth in her act:

> **You don't realise that when a baby pops out the front, a great big pile pops out the back.**

She also had a complete routine about her later hysterectomy. But she did not include divorce in her act - it was too painful.

> *I still felt like a mother but not a wife,* she said.

> **Did the earth move? No, but the wardrobe door came open.**

The Wood-Durham family moved to No 22 Stankelt Road, Silverdale, across Morecambe Bay from the town, later moving to Cove Lea, also in Silverdale. They kept a flat in North London, but later decided that to have as much time as possible with their growing children they would all have to live in London where Vic and Geoff inevitably spent a lot of time.

More from Stan's Journal, 31st January 1980:

> *One of Victoria's remarks, arising out of the women's programme* Pandora's Box *- I know I have ovaries but I don't want to write a song about them.*

5th February 1980 Tuesday:

Vicks is at Granada working on Daughter of Talent.

Even after she married Geoff, it was several years before Vic would wear a wedding ring. When the children came along, Grace in 1988 and Henry in 1992, Vic added pregnancy and childbirth to her stand-up routine. Interviewed by Gloria Hunniford on *Wogan* in 1991, Vic said that

taking a young child on the road was like having a baby chimp with you.

She then did a whole comedy routine, off the cuff I guess, about taking a pregnancy test.

Too shy to ask the chemist what she wanted, she first came away with a packet of aspirins. Finally obtaining the 'ovulation predictor kit' (Vic made even that prosaic name sound funny) she discovers she has to 'pee on a paddle', which she did with some difficulty.

We have the engine capacity but not the steering

quipped Vic to gales of laughter. Even the thoroughly professional Hunniford found it hard not to fall about laughing.

Wiki says:

Wood fiercely maintained her privacy and that of her children, even originally refusing to release publicly the name of her son when he was born.

Victoria Newton of *The Mail* wrote:

Victoria was never 'very keen' on getting married, and for years she even refused to wear a wedding ring. She once said: 'Being a wife never appealed to me and I was so embarrassed when I got married that I didn't tell anyone for two years. Geoff and I had been together for four years and he was asking me every day. We'd met when I was only twenty-three and I thought at the time I'd better keep my options open, but I didn't find anyone I liked nearly as much and never have, and eventually felt I was ready to do the honest thing.

Despite being considerably more successful than her husband, she has always insisted it was never a problem: 'People assume that if a woman is more famous than a man there's a problem in the marriage, but not at all,' she said, 'We sorted it out between us.' Last year [2001] she also said 'she had never been tempted to go looking elsewhere for love. In an interview before going on her latest tour, she said: 'Geoff and I have been through so much. I'm proud of the fact that we've been through so many different ways of living, done so many things, had so many ups and downs and we're still here to tell the tale. There has never been anyone else who could match him as far as I'm concerned, so there's never been an incentive to look elsewhere'.

The Smiths lead singer Morrissey, who greatly admired Vic's work, once joked that he wanted to marry her. She responded, in jokey fashion of course:

Morrissey and I have been married for eleven months, though due to touring commitments, we have yet to meet.

But reality kicked in when, in 2002, Victoria and Geoff split up and subsequently divorced. There was no-one else involved, and the parting was equally traumatic for both of them: two people I loved.

A friend said:

> Geoffrey has been a real rock for Victoria over the years, but they had drifted apart so far they felt it best to go their separate ways.

In 2011, Vic told *The Telegraph's* Chrissy Iley:

> I am divorced. I've been divorced for years. It was horrible, hideous, I wouldn't recommend it. He's in another relationship. I don't want to talk about him.

That wasn't because she harboured any ill-feeling towards her ex-husband, it was because she always found the subject of their divorce too painful to discuss. Her divorce was one of the few things that Vic did not use in her comedy routines.

Stuart Jeffries of the *Guardian* wrote:

> In 2002, her twenty-two year marriage ended. She told an interviewer in 2011 she had not been in another relationship since. There's not much of a chance for me finding somebody of my age. Gentlemen of my age are dropping down thirty years to find girlfriends.

That's not always the case, the interviewer replied.

> You're right. I need to get out of the house, she said.

When Vic and Geoff separated it was a huge shock to everybody. They'd been together for twenty-six years and seemed ideally matched. There is no doubt that the separation and subsequent divorce was hugely painful to both of them. Vic went into therapy.

One thing is certain: there was no-one else involved for either. Vic's publicist issued a statement:

Victoria Wood and Geoffrey Durham have with great sadness decided to separate. The separation is entirely amicable - there are no other parties involved.

Geoffrey moved out, but literally just round the corner. He continued to be a close and caring father for Grace and Henry, then fourteen and ten respectively, as has been the case ever since. It's a telling fact that, in her final illness, the 'close family' that Vic wanted around her were her children, Grace and Henry, her closest sister Rosalind, and ex-husband Geoff. That speaks volumes for the mutual respect and affection that Vic and Geoff had for one another even after the divorce.

In later years, with Rosalind and Victoria both living in London, Penelope in Yorkshire and me in County Durham, it was not surprising that the two youngest were the closest of us four siblings. As Victoria made the sad and painful journey through her final illness, Rosalind, along with Grace, Henry and ex-husband Geoff, gave every possible care to their beloved Vic.

With *dinnerladies* I was particularly pleased to see that, for once, Vic had written a part for herself that included love and even the possibility of sex. Her character had a touching, down-to-earth romance with the canteen manager Tony played by Andrew Dunn. The only other time I can think of when this happened was in Vic's 1994 TV film *Pat and Margaret*. Vic plays the dumpy, dowdy waitress sister of glamorous US soap star Julie Walters who are briefly reunited after twenty-seven years.

Duncan Preston plays Vic's mild-mannered boyfriend Jim whose dragon of a mother (Thora Hird) is utterly disgusted to discover that the young couple have had sex, not only in her house, but also in her bedroom. 'It was only on the bed, not in it' says Jim, to which his mother, greatly disgusted, replies 'NOT on my best eiderdown!' No-one could do disgust just like Thora, who declared later 'that was one of my favourite lines'. Vic always wrote for her actors, and here she hit the spot exactly. Hird was one of a number of older actresses, including particularly Anne Reid and Thelma Barlow, that Vic admired and included in her work whenever she could.

A few of Vic's real-life outbursts were directed at me. On watching *Pat and Margaret* I was much moved, as there were echoes for me, a complete unknown if not an 'ordinary' bloke, being the sibling of a superstar. I made the mistake of mentioning this to one of my other sisters. Within hours, Vic was on the 'phone, all guns blazing.

> *How dare you compare my film with our situation? This is a work of FICTION. It has NOTHING WHATEVER to do with you and me!*

I could only mumble that I was not making a direct comparison, but that I was affected by the film, which, as with all Vic's work, I thought was excellent. But madam was not to be mollified. My fault - I should have kept my thoughts to myself.

In 2011, Chrissy Iley of *The Telegraph* interviewed Victoria:

> *We are here to talk about the play she has written, and is directing,* That Day We Sang. *The highlight of the Manchester International Festival, it's about a famous recording of Purcell's* Nymphs and Shepherds *made by the Manchester Children's Choir - a group of 250 working-class children - in 1929 and their subsequent reunion in 1969. The choir existed, so did the reunion, which was filmed by*

Granada Television, but everything else is fiction.

Basically it's the story of two middle-aged people, Tubby and Enid, who meet again in 1969,' says Wood. 'I didn't have to research much of it because I was there. (She's from Bury and was sixteen in 1969). I talked to two ladies who were in the choir. They were ninety-two and ninety-five.' Iley wrote: *'The characters in her play, Tubby and Enid, are also shy and the play explores how they confront their shyness when, as middle-aged people, they meet each other after forty years. 'I saw a documentary, which I thought was Granada, in about 1975, and I remembered it for years,' says Wood. 'Then they found it for me and I watched it, and it was nothing like I remembered it. I'd invented the whole documentary in my head. It was strange, but that was the starting point'.*

Iley goes on:

The play is typical Wood: tragicomic, filled with achingly observed minutiae. Only Victoria Wood could have several minutes of successful dialogue devoted to yogurts and their slimming properties. Yogurts were peaking in 1969. She grins. 'Yogurts had to taste horrible or it wasn't slimming. Remember Ski? It was 11p in my day.' But more of that later. In the play, Wood says, Tubby is, 'trying to get a romance going in a very sensitive way, and what he doesn't know is that she's having an affair with the boss. He's making advances and she's rebuffing him and he doesn't know why.' She smiles, giggles nervously even, at the potential tragedy.

I once went to one of those parties where everyone throws their car keys into the middle of the room. I don't know

who got my moped but I've been driving that Peugeot for years.

For me, the highlight of Vic's stand-up stage show was always her rendition of *The Ballad of Barry and Freda*. The relentless build-up, with verse after verse of sparkling lines, leading to the climax 'Be mighty. Be flighty. Come and melt the buttons on my flameproof nightie' was almost too much to bear. Time after time, I would ask myself 'can she really lift the audience to such an extreme pitch?' But she did - every single time.

The 'question and response' format of the song has been often used in gospel music, comedy songs such as *There's a Hole in My Bucket*, and with Ray Charles' hits like *What'd I Say* and *Hit the Road Jack*. Knowing that there is going to be this dual effect in every verse only makes it all the more compelling. With so much of our culture predicated on sex-hungry males chasing hard-to-get females, Vic reverses that by having a love-hungry wife making demands on her (very) reluctant husband. That is Vic's genius.

Freda bombards Barry with ever-increasingly desperate pleas for a night of uninhibited marital sex, while Barry responds with equally ever-increasing desperate pleas to be excused. Freda:

> ***I'm on fire with desire - I could handle half the tenors in a male voice choir;***

To which the harassed and fearful Barry can only reply

> ***I can't do it!***

Vic could have gone on indefinitely, doing her stand-up and delighting packed houses with *The Ballad of Barry and Freda*. But when she had done one thing to the fullest extent, she wanted to move on to another. For Victoria Wood, there were always more fields to conquer. But *Barry and Freda* remains an enduring favourite with her millions of fans.

After Vic's death, Louis Barfe of *The Express* wrote:

> *The comedian was shy and a very private person off-stage As an example of her shyness, only producer Geoff Posner saw her rehearse* The Ballad of Barry and Freda, *the song best known to most people as* Let's Do It! *Everyone else saw it first on the dress run. On the recording, Posner asked for a second take. She demurred, explaining that they wouldn't laugh the second time. 'I squeezed her hand and asked if she was OK,' Gould recalls. 'She did the number again and the audience laughed even louder. We still used take one.'*

"Up to you Porky!"

CHAPTER FOUR

UP TO YOU, PORKY!

One of the many reasons I admire Vic is the way that she dealt with negative personal comments. Not only did she accommodate it in her own life, she used it in her stand-up performances and in her TV comedy shows.

Vic said: 'I was always very upset if they ever said I was fat - even though I was. I felt they shouldn't mention it. I felt it wasn't relevant, but of course it's a British obsession. I was patronised either for being fat, for being a woman or for being northern. I just felt I was living in a world of mad southern people'.

Vic never fully overcame this particular demon - she herself admitted it was always with her - but she conquered her weight problem and kept it under control with sensible eating and regular exercise. More than that, Vic made a public show of the overweight girl and was never afraid of using her own body to illustrate her unique brand of comedy. There was the girl making a forlorn attempt to swim the Channel without backup, and the manic fitness instructor who was super-keen but clearly unfit.

And where has it got you, having a pelvic floor like a bulldog clip?

In her sketch *Welcome to Fattitude* Vic plays Madge, an aerobic instructor wearing a pink lycra bodysuit and what she calls 'my flattering new leotard'. Madge says: 'Have you not got any trainers? Well, just do your best in those. They're not ideal, though, stilettos. Warming up... Marching on the spot [with vigorous marching by Vic] both legs, Connie.' Seeing this hilarious sketch on stage several times, I found some of the audience laughter a little strained. Maybe it was a bit too near the truth for some.

Another of Vic's characters was about a woman on a diet who makes a panic telephone call to a help-line when she is out shopping because she has been brought 'face to face with a Marks & Spencer's individual spotted dick'.

Stan was well ahead of his child prodigy in making fun of fatness. In 1939 he had a book of Lancashire dialect comic verse published by Samuel French. In it Stan features the overweight cleaner Mrs Clutterbuck who needs an oversize gas mask to cover her five chins. She leaves No. 10 Downing Street with a note on the door 'Spring Cleaning, Back Next Week', and goes to Germany to give Hitler a clip round the ear.

31st January 1970:

> *Vicky goes out with Bob Mason. Wife said: 'Their babies will be like balloons'. V said: 'We're going to get married, you know, when I'm twenty-three'. She is going to meet his parents.*

> **I've always been big. When I was born I didn't go into a cot, I went straight into a bunk.**

Victoria made her two-programme *Victoria Wood's Big Fat Documentary* for BBC1 in 2003, transmitted in January the following year. It's a critique of the dieting industry, about which Vic was highly critical. *Up To You, Porky!* is the title of Victoria's book of her sketches, published in 1985. She chose the title, another indication that Vic was only too willing to make fun of herself being overweight, even though it had caused her great personal unhappiness over the years. *Up To You, Porky!* is a line from one of Vic's sketches (from *VWASOT*) in which she, as a normal-sized woman, goes into a fashion boutique where all the models are stick thin.

The assistant, played by Julie Walters, is scathing. When Vic as the customer asks if she has something in a size fourteen, Julie is incredulous: 'You what? This is a boutique, not the Elephant House! [to a colleague] Hey, Eileen, got another Fatso in!' When Vic asks to try something on, Julie's response is '*Up to you, Porky!*'

A preview by *Weight Loss Resources* said:

Victoria Wood's new documentary series promises to be lively and contentious as well as giving us all a chance to laugh at the Big Fat subject. Billed as a personal and honest take on the dieting industry, the Big Fat Documentary *follows Victoria's investigation into media pressure, fat acceptance, slimming products, diet fads and the history of the ideal body shape. On Victoria's amusing journey she attempts to answer such questions as: why is it hard to lose weight? Why are slimming clubs in such horrible halls? Why have we become a nation of overeaters? 'I've started enough diets in my life to understand that buzz you get from weighing out a quarter cup of muesli, four ounces of skimmed milk and a dried apricot,' she says. 'But I'm hugely entertained by the madness of it all.' Helping Victoria along the way are exercise gurus, dieting experts and a smattering of celebrities including the Duchess of York, Vanessa Feltz and Anne Robinson.*

Yet Vic's decision to use her own weight problem in her comedy was not taken lightly. In 2001 she told *The Telegraph*:

I've never let it get so near to my own experience before. This is based on what actually happened to me. I wasn't scared to do it any more. I wasn't trying to hide behind something. I've got nothing to prove and I wanted to grant myself the freedom to talk about what I wanted to talk about. It's not a confessional and it's not therapy, it is just jokes, but it is very rooted in what I've just been doing. I can only tell jokes about something if I've totally come to terms with it anyway. So I could never have said 'I have an eating problem' until I'd sorted it through for myself.

Vic often said that food, especially sweets, was her consolation. Producer Jude Kelly, who studied drama at Birmingham University with Victoria, recalled that she 'ate a lot of chocolate'. Perhaps it's apocryphal, but it has been said that Vic, or her mother, or both, kept a drawer full of Curly-Wurlys - for emergency use only! She would never admit if either was true, but I suspect it was.

In 2007 Rachel Halliburton of *The Independent* found a fit-looking Victoria talking a lot about having grown in confidence:

She is 'happy' with who she is, unlike the younger Wood who 'spent time as a teenager getting hold of rolls of fat and looking in the mirror and just despising myself', said Halliburton.

In *VWASOTV* Vic gave herself the line:

> *I'm not the body beautiful. I've done for fitness what Norman Fowler [Secretary of State for Social Services 1981-87] has done for the NHS.*

In 2014, Victoria told Richard Barber of the *Mail*:

> *That after years of obsessing about her weight, she had arrived at a size with which she was comfortable. 'I'm not a cook. I'm just not interested. I haven't cooked properly since Henry [her son] left home. If I go to restaurants, it's to meet friends. I'd never go for the cuisine. I was brought up on boring food. I never liked my mother's cooking. My memory is of sitting at the table staring at a carrot I didn't want to eat and being made to sit there until I did. I was only ever interested in chocolates and sweets. I couldn't understand people who wanted to sit down and have dinner and a chat and eat slowly. I felt I wanted to eat a lot and preferably in private.*

Written for *Wood and Walters*, Vic first sang *What We Find* at the Bolton Festival. It includes these lines: 'swim for health, splash about, the chorine makes your hair fall out' and 'You rub your necks before you sleep with cream that's made from bits of sheep. Is this wise? Are you mad? Is it kind?'

Barber said Victoria developed a tolerance for exercising in her later years.

> *I do twenty press-ups every morning, and if I'm not working I work out, either at home or in the gym. I like to go on a treadmill and watch the telly at the same time. It can't be anything too subtle, though. I enjoyed something called Paralysed And Pregnant With Twins (2010), and I also liked*

Half Ton Dad (2008) about the fattest man in the world having bits chopped off him. I watched through my fingers - quite a high-risk strategy if you're on a moving treadmill!

Frances Hardy of The *Mail* interviewed Victoria in 2009. Hardy wrote that Vic looked 'toned and fit' in a lumberjack shirt, jeans and trainers.

In my 20s I was going around seeing agents who were patronising because I was fat and a girl, which was a double whammy,' said Vic, who once observed that jogging was for people who weren't intelligent enough to watch television, but now runs occasional marathons and adheres to the sort of strict fitness regime she would have once mocked as risibly draconian. 'I have a treadmill at home for my cardio-workout and then I go to the gym for a proper big workout with weights', said Vic, 'I do it under supervision - one-to-one - or I wouldn't work hard enough', hinting at having a personal trainer.

Is she blonde? What are her vital statistics? (local journalist)

There is no doubt that Vic was sensitive about her weight, especially in the early years. That led to one of the few 'spats' that she and I had over the years. Most brothers and sisters argue at some point, so I guess four or five times in forty-plus years as adults isn't bad. Our first came in 1974 when Victoria won her heat of *New Faces*. Naturally I was immensely proud of her success and let everybody know about it. This reached the ears of a local journalist, who rang me up.

'I hear your sister has won *New Faces*,' he said, 'is she blonde? What are her vital statistics?' Clearly he had not seen the programme. Then I made two mistakes. Wanting to help a fellow journalist, and (I thought) a friend, I told him

Victoria is not blonde. She's not a beauty queen. She's more on the plump side.

And - stupid man that I was - I gave him her telephone number. I never made either mistake again!

Your brother says you're fat!

He then rang Victoria and told her: 'Your brother says you're fat!' I was in trouble. Deep, deep trouble. Victoria (remember, she was still only twenty-one) spat back: 'How does he know? He hasn't seen me for five years!' Of course that just wasn't true. I'd met up with Vic - happily, and at her suggestion - two or three times while she was at Birmingham University, and also when she was on tour with Jasper Carrott. So I'd certainly seen her in the previous few months. But she was hurt, caught off guard and responded with the sort of quip that was her comedy trademark.

In 1976 Vic had a season on Esther Rantzen's TV show *That's Life*. It was recorded on Sundays. Rantzen would ring Vic on a Friday with that week's topic. It earned Vic £30 each fortnight and enabled her to buy a minivan. Vic was also on the BBC's *Start the Week*, and was getting more bookings including three nights at the London ICA. She played in the review *In at the Death* at the Bush Theatre, London, July 13th to August 6th 1978. Director Dusty Hughes saw Vic's show at the ICA. She had reviews in *The Daily Telegraph*, the *West London Observer* and *Time Out*. At the Bush, Vic wrote the sketch *Sex* about a girl who thinks she is pregnant but has never had sex.

Vic said that this was the first time she fully realised how to make something funny. She said:

> This sketch. It was called Sex - Julie was a librarian, and I was a woman getting a book out. Alison Fiske, who played a sort of happyish, middle-aged woman comes in and this girl says, 'I think I'm pregnant', and she says, 'Where are you in the menstrual cycle?' And she says, 'Taurus'. And that was the first - that was like a proper joke, boom boom, it's a joke, you know.

There were good reviews in the *Financial Times* and the *Sunday Telegraph*. David Leland, director at the Crucible, Sheffield, was also impressed.

Guardian drama critic Michael Billington wrote:

> The one talent that does emerge well out of the show [In At The Death] is that of the song and sketch writer Victoria Wood. She has a couple of very good numbers about Guy the Gorilla and a middle-class woman who can't be bothered to visit her mother in a home ('You don't know how I envy you, not a thing to do all day'): jaunty tunes combined with mordant lyrics. And Miss Wood is also the author of the one sure-fire sketch, Sex, in which women express their distaste for the male organ and which also contains the classic line, from a girl defending herself against a shop-lifting charge, 'A duvet fell into my shopping bag'. Dusty Hughes has edited and directed the show. He has got some good performers here, including Miss Wood, Alison Fiske and Julie Walters.

Vic wrote *Love Song* for the Bush revue. She said it was her only sad song:

Made your breakfast this morning like any old day. Then I remembered and threw it away.

But she also wrote *The Song of the Lonely Girl*, *I've had it up to here* and other bitter-sweet songs. (*Lucky Bag*).

In my 20s I was going round seeing agents who were patronising me because I was fat and a girl.

In an interview with Richard E Grant, Vic said:

I can pinpoint when I realised how you wrote a joke. And that was unfortunate, because I'd been in comedy for seven years already! The first ever sketch I wrote, when I was at the Bush Theatre in 1978, when I first realised I could actually form a joke on a piece of paper, was a fantastic day. I wrote a sketch for me and Julie. And just a voice and a way of talking came into my head, and a way of phrasing, and all the things that an outsider would say 'That's very Victoria Wood', just came out. And it was like when you struck a gong and it's true. And I thought, that's it, that's it then. I pity the poor people who saw me before then!

Vic's stage musical *Talent* had an eighteen night run from January 31st 1979. There was a poor crit by *The Telegraph*, but other reviews were better. Producer Peter Eckersley bought *Talent* for Granada, and Vic was on her way. As well as scaling the peaks of showbiz, Vic also (eventually) overcame her weight problem.

My career didn't take off so much as to reverse into the departure lounge.

By 1990 Charles Spencer, the then deputy theatre critic of *The Telegraph* but soon to start a twenty-five year stint as head theatre critic before retiring in 2016, was able to write about a 'glowingly self-confident woman' who had lost weight. He said: 'Success suits Victoria Wood. Like Miss Jean Brodie she is in her prime. Her show, *Up West* at the Strand Theatre, has entirely sold out its ten week run (find a friendly tout) and it is hard to square the glowingly self-confident woman on stage with the diffident fattie who cut her comic teeth in the cramped surroundings of the King's Head in the early eighties. But while Ms Wood has lost weight she has lost none of her powers of often malicious observation. In the course of her two-hour show, she scarcely puts a foot wrong. It's a great night, but not one for either the squeamish or male DIY enthusiasts'.

In 2012 Vic told Chrissy Iley of *The Telegraph* that she used to eat all the time. 'I was never hungry. You're not if you eat all the time. You never get that scary feeling of hunger. You want your mind to be distracted. You want to put a wall between you and real life. It's like the drink or the fags or the drugs. It's all the same. Some people have addictive natures and some people have odd relationships with food. I do have an addictive nature, but it's manageable'.

In 1993 Vic found she had an allergy to sugar. Dealing with that, plus Jane Fonda workouts, press-ups, swimming and power walking, did the trick. Vic slimmed down and maintained a healthy weight thereafter. In August 1990 *Best Magazine* said: 'Victoria Wood: she lost two stones over two years, mainly through exercise. 'Half of me thought, it's not really important what you look like; the other half used to be really embarrassed by the fact that it was always mentioned' says the now average sized comedienne'.

Perhaps the last word on managing her weight should rest

with Vic herself. 'Moving on, I could never have said 'I have an eating problem' until I'd sorted it out myself', she told *The Telegraph's* Jasper Rees in 2001:

> *I haven't got a waist. I've just got a sort of place. A bit like an unmarked level crossing.*

Vic sent Keith Waterhouse a fan letter, and she wrote to Peter Ustinov and Willie Rushton asking for advice. Ustinov had none; Rushton didn't reply. She was working at a bar near the Pebble Mill studios when a couple of producers found out she was a musician and invited her to audition. She thought it was a joke. Next day, there was telephone call from the BBC: 'we're here waiting for you to audition. Where are you?' She dashed around, played the piano and was hired to play musical numbers for their regional programmes.

In 1974 the twenty-one year old Victoria was in her final year of her drama degree course at Birmingham University when she first appeared on national television in *New Faces*, a show produced by ATV for the ITV network. First screened in 1973, *New Faces* was a talent show, the seventies equivalent of *X-Factor* or *Britain's Got Talent*. A panel of four judges gave the contestants marks for content, presentation and star quality.

Auditions for *New Faces* were held at the La Dolce Vita Nightclub in Birmingham on Saturday October 12th 1974. Victoria applied, was accepted and - perhaps surprisingly - she won her heat to gain a place in the all winners show. She didn't win that, but was invited to take part in a spin-off programme *Summer Show*, five forty-five minute shows with Jack Parnell and his Orchestra. She got £75 for each *New Faces* programme. The programme blurb said: 'Victoria Wood...claims to be able to write a song on any subject in an hour and a half'.

Victoria said that she got a friend of hers who worked at ATV to put her application on top of the pile (*Victoria Wood - Seen On TV* 2009) but I would take that with a pinch of salt. Even if it was true, would it really have helped get her on the show? TV producer Paul Stewart Laing said it was all thanks to one of the programme's make-up ladies. 'She used to nag all the time, 'you've got to see this girl, she's so funny'. Her sister was at Birmingham University [not correct] with Victoria and she thought she ought to have a chance on a talent show. So eventually after a lot of nagging - I'm glad that we did - she came onto *New Faces* and she won it... she obviously went on to bigger things.

But she was eliminated in the second round, in which she sang a song called *Lorraine* about a woman dolefully contemplating marriage to a man who washes his Cortina more than his neck. Even though she didn't make the *New Faces* final, she was selected to join the comedian Lenny Henry and singer-comedian Marti Caine to appear in the *Summer Show*, a variety series fronted by Leslie Crowther, in which she wore a bustle and duetted with the host.

> *By God, if her bum were a bungalow she'd never get a mortgage on it.*

Stan kept a newspaper cutting:

> The seven faces of success. Look out for some familiar faces in the *Summer Show*. All are successes from *New Faces*. They are, from left, Nicky Martin, compere, comedian, singer, dancer, ukulele player; the winner of *New Faces* All Winners Gala Final, singer/comedienne Marti Caine ('as a

child I was a singer, always doing concert parties and pantomimes. The comedy came when I started talking...'); Aiden J Harvey, impressionist and winner of the all winners show in July last year; Charlie James, pretty 4ft 7in female singer with the big South Wales voice; Lenny Henry, sixteen year old impressionist who has three ambitions - to make the big time, to give his parents a Jamaican holiday, and then take his GCE 'O' Levels; Victoria Wood, happy songwriter and comedienne from Ramsbottom, Manchester; and Trevor Chance, the Cumberland singer who was the first ever *New Faces* winner. With Jack Parnell and his Orchestra.

A not too serious look at 'Kids' in this week's theme, presented by the versatile music and comedy team. The songs include *Father of Girls*; *In My Little Snapshot Album*; *All Fingers and Thumbs*; and Marti Caine's latest release *Momma's Song.* In the sketches, favourites from children's television are featured, including a musical version of *Star Trek*. The writers are Bryan Blackburn, Dick Vosburgh and Tony Hawes. The musical associate is Derek Scott. Designer: Paul Dean Fortune; director Peter Harris; Producer Colin Clews. ATV Network Production.

After her TV appearance on *New Faces* and *That's Life*, Vic thought she would be famous very soon. But is was not like that at all. Thanks to her naively signing up with 'an ex-bandleader from Hove who contrived to turn down every offer of work', she found herself living in a £13 a week bedsit drinking milk out of a bottle and eating biscuits. Vic said:

I used to be really boring. I had no proper material, just a selection of pathetic songs. I used to get a booking every six months and die a death.

91

Vic felt she was:

All washed up at the age of twenty-three. When I started off I had a completely inflated idea of my own talent. I was very ambitious and very clueless. I remember saying to myself, I'm going to make a start and it may take twenty minutes or it may take a couple of hours, but it will happen very shortly. But the reality was cabaret in Solihull: singing to people gnawing at chicken legs - because they only stop for the star.

Of *New Faces*, Vic said:

Strangely it wasn't ultimately very good for me. I was twenty-one and straight out of university. All I could do was write little songs. I went on, they thought 'Marvellous' but that was all I could do. My whole act was about three minutes long! Then I made a lot of classic mistakes like signing up with management and publishers. With the publishers deal I had given them 50% of my royalty earnings. Mind you, I think they ended up with only about three shillings and sixpence so it served them right! I also had a very odd manager who turned down every job I was offered unless it was on TV. Consequently I did quite a lot of TV, but they were always short spots. Whenever I did get a live date I was diabolical because I hadn't learned what I was supposed to be doing. Appearing on That's Life *was another break I could have made better use of. I was incredibly naïve. If I had had some sort of mentor I wouldn't have made those mistakes.*

My nose has grown so big, the rest of my face is applying for a council flat.

She advertised her own self-promoted show *Tickling My Ivories - An Evening with Victoria Wood:* An evening of singing, talking, sketches, standing up, sitting down again, and possibly one card trick. It is available for theatres, community centres, arts festivals and cabaret. All enquiries Victoria Wood 12 Oxford Street Morecambe Lancs LA4 5JF (0524) 417092 24-hour answering service.

Vic 'too anxious' to read reviews, but asked Geoff to read the best ones. In 1977 Vic appeared on the Granada TV programme *Pandora's Box* with Joan Bakewell. Again, Vic wrote and sang her own songs linked with each edition.

Stan noted in his Journal: 9-10th August 1975 Saturday/Sunday:

> Summer Show *was much better than we expected. Sketches, songs & musical backing all much improved and more professional. I recorded most of it.*

11th July 1977 Monday:

> *Vicky home composing madly - seven songs for Granada, £50 a song & £30 fee. Mama typing thesis.*

5th August 1979 Sunday:

> *Vicky's musical* Talent *went out without a hitch. She was splendid and obviously a smash hit. All the Nationals had rave reviews either before or after, some both. Compared to the live stage version, the TV version had obviously been opened out & it lost tension. But the TV version was beautiful & exciting to watch - two superb actresses, perfect foils for each other. The songs were great: Julie, I wish I was fourteen again, Me In the Evening, Pals.*

9th August 1979 Thursday:

This evening we took V & Geoff to dine at the Mason's Arms. It was excellent in every way. They arrived about 5pm. We had tea & biscuits & jolly chat. V & G wandered over the fields. Glad the fuss is dying down. She is not to give any more interviews until Oct when her current play should be finished. She will do two more Maureen & Julie ones for Granada.

Famous for three minutes, out of work for two years

But Stan had his own writing success.

12th January 1980 *Radio Times*:

Radio 4 UK 2.30 stereo Saturday Afternoon Theatre Summer of 28 by Stanley Wood, with Christian Rodska, directed by Tony Cliff, BBC Manchester.

13-14th January 1980:

Still in a state of euphoria.

7th April 1980:

Vicky's play Good Fun well received. Good notices Daily Express, Guardian etc.

15th April 1980:

Good news from Geoff. Leland, V's director of Good Fun, has been sacked. Peter James will now produce. Leland goes end of June. Show goes back to Sheffield in July with new Director, but Leland's name will still appear in some face-saving arrangement, (still by print). Vicky & Geoff are doing concerts (solo) May 4th Halifax 11th & possibly 17th? Talent opens in New York & Philadelphia. V & G go to New York to advise.

19th April 1980 Saturday:

Ticket for Good Fun *at the Crucible Theatre.*

Lancashire Evening Post, 26th May 1980:

Miss Wood was the girl who wrote and co-starred in the musical play Talent *, and in this weekend's follow-up* Nearly a Happy Ending *(ITV 9.30) she plays the same character. In her own script, she made the girl lose more than two stone in weight, so there was nothing for it but for Victoria the actress to do what Victoria the writer demanded. She went into a regime of early morning swims and tonic water booze-ups, encouraged all the way by the rest of the* Happy Ending *cast. Now Victoria, two and a half stone less cuddly than she was when we last saw her, intends to stay the shape she is. Hopefully too, this new musical - to be followed next year with yet another adventure in the lives of Julie the pretty one and her fat friend Maureen - will prove as popular as* Talent. *That has already won three major awards, was short-listed for several others, and is still in the running for more.*

1st June 1980 Sunday:

Almost a Happy Ending. V & G have seen rough version & like it very much. Also, at last they have found the LP company they have been looking for - it is Pye.

Arrangements by Jim Parker, director Norman Newall. V is only just about making ends meet on £100 a week in Sheffield. She will get £300 a week in London & 5% of the takings until the show breaks even & then 10% which is very good. G says V is on top of the world but needs a holiday. Also she is hardening towards critics. The two worst reviews were the New Statesman *& the* Observer. *All the rest very laudatory.*

Is there anything Victoria Wood cannot do? The Times

The *Times* 18th January 1982:

Is there anything Victoria Wood cannot do? She writes witty lyrics and sets them charmingly to music. She has a sweet voice, and a relaxed and professional touch as a self-accompanist on the piano. She writes hilarious sketches, and had notched up two good plays. She has a telegenic face, and on stage has that rare ability to catch and hold an audience. She is a first-class comic actress... Last night's edition of Wood and Walters *(Granada) amply fulfilled the promise of its pilot a couple of weeks ago: the old collaboration has never worked better.*

" Two Soups? "

97

CHAPTER FIVE

TWO SOUPS

Victoria Wood was dubbed the 'Queen of Comedy' by the *Sunday Post* in December 1986 after starring in the previous month's *Royal Variety Show*. I have so much respect and admiration for my sister: not only did she become the nation's favourite and best-loved comedian, she did it entirely her way, with her own unique brand of comedy.

Many people have said that the characters Victoria portrayed in her sketches were based on real people. Vic always denied this, but there is no doubt whatsoever that she had a keen eye for observation and a very retentive memory. Things she saw and ideas she came up with would be squirreled away and brought forward - sometimes years later - to be used on stage or on TV. With such a prodigious output over forty or more years, it was just as well.

What has pleased the public and critics alike is that her characters, so memorable, mostly amusing but also often dramatic, are undoubtedly based on real life. We all know people at least a little bit like 'char' Mrs Overall or the painfully slow, forgetful waitress in *Two Soups*. It is being based on reality, however distorted or exaggerated when seen through Victoria's unique prism, that endears us so much to her wonderful creations.

Two Soups Director Geoff Posner told *The Telegraph*:

> *There were three of us sat on the floor in a little cottage in North West England - Victoria, Julie Walters and myself. It was 1984; I was a young producer, having just made* The Young Ones *and the pilot of* Blackadder, *and had seen Victoria in a play called* Good Fun. *When I heard she'd been signed up to the BBC, to make a series called* As Seen On TV, *I asked if I could work on it. The series was for BBC2, which I could never fathom. But back then it was never considered that she would be mainstream.*
>
> *We were reading Vic's scripts, although I didn't do any reading: we'd get to a sketch and Julie would say 'Who's this, Vic?' The characters were always based on someone the two of them had met - Vic would say 'It's that waitress from that cafe', or 'do you remember that lady from the supermarket?' and Julie would immediately give a hysterical reading of every person in the scene. At the end of it, Victoria looked up to me and said timidly 'Was it alright?' Alright? I felt spoiled to be there.*

The 1985 *WVASOTV* sketch *Two Soups*, featuring Julie Walters as a doddery and forgetful waitress, with Celia Imrie and Duncan Preston as diners in a hurry, is now widely regarded as a classic. Even on the night it was recorded it was clearly something very special. 'The audience reaction in the studio was immense. I've never heard laughter like it,' recalled production manager and later director Roy Gould. Vic said in the read through that

> *it looks rubbish on the page, but just wait until Jules [Julie Walters] does it. Jules just marked it all week in rehearsals and then went for it on the recording. I actually bit into my*

bottom lip and drew blood to stop myself from corpsing. I was trying to keep out of Celia's eyeline as I could see her going.

An unexpected problem with Vic's TV shows was that the rest of the cast found it very difficult to keep a straight face as they played the characters Vic gave them. Quite often recordings would be halted as her fellow actors fell about laughing.

The BBC's Geoff Posner (producer of *The Young Ones, Blackadder, French and Saunders, Little Britain*) recalled:

Then there was the time when, in Acorn Antiques, the cast were all bunched up on a sofa and Mrs Overall made an appearance in a pair of lumpy tights no-one had ever seen before. Every time we went for a take, the cast could feel each others' shoulders moving and couldn't contain the wails of laughter. It took about half an hour to get it.

Posner told *The Telegraph*:

Working in comedy, you normally become immune and the joke gets less funny the more times you hear it, but Vic and Julie seemed to be infinitely funny and the crew would have to try and contain themselves shooting it. At one point, our cameraman actually dropped the camera when Julie, acting the role of a hairdresser to a comic, said the line 'Of course, prior to this, I was a man'.

Posner said:

Her work arrived fully formed, exactly the right length and filled with her amazing view of the world. They were like poems that had to be delivered in a certain cadence so that they would land exactly where they were supposed to: Victoria wrote every single word of all the projects we did together. When I said to her 'who'll write the music?' she said, 'I already have'. When we came to recording the theme tune of Acorn Antiques, *she pulled out her very own Stylophone.*

Jogging is for people who aren't intelligent enough to watch television.

Many years earlier, long before he became a scriptwriter on *Coronation Street*, Dad explained to me the importance of a 'back story' for the individual characters in the first episode of a serial or sitcom series. 'Every character in a radio or television series starts in episode one with a history. It's important that the scriptwriters and actors know what that history is', he said. I have no doubt Dad also passed this on to Vic. Her characters appear fully formed with their own history, implied if not told directly.

It was at Birmingham that Victoria developed the idea of writing and performing topical and comic songs, accompanying herself on the piano. She found a slot on local radio, and linked up with Jasper Carrott and Roger McGough. Vic said that from 1974 to 1978 she worked 'on and off' at folk clubs and late night theatres.

Carrott, eight years older than Vic, ran a folk club in Solihull where he was MC and also performed. Like Billy Connolly, his patter between songs developed into stand-up comedy. Carrott also had a hit record in 1975 with *Funky Moped* b/w *The Magic Roundabout*. That year he went on tour with Victoria as support, and I caught the show at Newcastle's City Hall and met both backstage afterwards.

By then Vic had already been tagged 'the female Jake

Thackray', a phrase she hated. 'Why don't they call him the male Victoria Wood?' she complained to me. Thackray was born in 1938. He spoke and sang in a strong Yorkshire accent, and recorded a folk album in 1969. From 1967 to 1972 he made regular appearances on the Bernard Braden's TV consumer programme *Braden's Week*, continuing with its successor programme *That's Life* presented by Esther Rantzen who had also appeared with Braden. In 1976 Victoria took over the 'topical song' slot from Thackray, so perhaps the media can be forgiven for making the comparison.

Roger McGough, born in Lancashire in 1937, was a 'performance poet' and a member of the Liverpool group Scaffold who had a hit comedy record with *Lily the Pink* in 1968. By then he was making regular appearances at the Edinburgh Festival, and it was at Edinburgh in 1975 that he and Victoria appeared in the *G.R.I.M.M.S* revue which later transferred to the Hampstead Theatre in London.

The following year Vic appeared in another revue at the Edinburgh Fringe, again devised and written by McGough, called *Wordplay*. Again it transferred from Edinburgh to the Hampstead Theatre. Michael Billington of the *Guardian* noted Vic's 'genial songs', and Irving Wardle of the *Times* highlighted 'the deadpan artist Victoria Wood' as one of the 'drollest personalities'.

Before Victoria broke through with her first play *Talent*, she found it hard going to establish herself as a performer. Despite appearing on television with *New Faces*, *Summer Show* and *That's Life*, Vic just wasn't getting the bookings on which she could build a career. This was due in large measure to the fact that she had signed up with an agent who simply was not up to the job.

Exactly why Vic committed herself to a three-year contract with a former bandleader in Hove, she herself could never explain. 'It's just the sort of thing that girls do' was all she could offer. For some inexplicable reason, this agent 'turned everything down'. Even her precious spot on *That's Life* only came about because Vic followed up the initial enquiry after her agent had failed to do so, rescuing the original letter from the bin.

Later on, Vic teamed up with Phil McIntyre from Lancaster who proved to be not only a first-class agent, but also a very good friend. Before that, Vic did whatever she could to get on a stage and entertain.

Performing with her husband, magician Geoffrey Durham, Vic worried about him more than herself. In 2002 she told *The Independent*'s Rachel Halliburton that she had strong memories of the days before she achieved national fame, when appearing in fringe venues was fraught with terrors. 'When I was working with my husband, I used to dread something going wrong with his show. Not that it ever did. But I used to sit in the toilet and flush it so I couldn't hear the audience'.

Ben Lawrence of *The Telegraph* asked Vic if she had ever been heckled: 'She thought hard. 'I don't think I have,' she said. 'At least not for a very long time. I remember someone shouting out 'I thought you'd be much taller.' This was Wood all over - she could make the mundane seem magical'.

Sexual harassment at work. Is it a problem for the self-employed?

I can remember Vic being heckled. It was at the City Hall in Newcastle when she appeared as support for comic Jasper Carrot. It was mainly a student audience, and they gave Vic a hard time. To her credit, she kept her composure, answered them back and carried on playing the piano and singing her songs. They quietened down.

Stan noted Vic's progress in his Journal: 22nd June 1975:

Victoria and friends (six of them) hope to find a farmhouse near Edinburgh. Vicky does a Song When I was four *holding up a photo of when she was four.*

31st August 1975:

We watched Vicky at Brighton (pub) and Forte Place, Newcastle, when rehearsing Black & White.

7th October 1976 Thursday:

Last night collected Victoria from the Old Swan, Harrogate, where she was appearing at banquet. The piano was awful and they took no notice of her feeble sallies! She got £75 though. She is looking forward to her forthcoming tour.

Lancashire Evening Post, May 1980:

Victoria Wood rounded off a week at the Lancaster Literary Festival with a hilarious performance which reduced a packed house to tears of joy. Her wickedly accurate ability to grab the sweat and smell of human relationships worked the audience into non-stop laughter. The award- winning dramatist and comedienne was superb. Morecambe, her home town, and the welcome departure from male-based jokes about sex, provided a suitable climax to a week's festival which has reinforced Lancaster's importance as a focal point in the entertainment calendar. It wasn't just a performance of original wit and stunning professionalism. The one-time professional actress conjured up those moments from childhood which lurk in all our memories. It must have been one of the happiest nights the Duke's Theatre has ever seen. Bucks Fizz [sic] were a splendid opening act. Their cabaret expertise was evident. Their humour and performance was elegant and hilarious, and several hundred people laughed through an unforgettable evening.

Stan's delight, 10th April 1981 Friday:

Victoria at the Royal Exchange, Manchester: A Date with Victoria Wood. Almost a full house. For one hour fifteen minutes she played and sang and joked with tremendous gusto, clarity, humour & professional panache. It was a stunning, exhilarating, spell-binding performance. I was delighted. Went backstage and embraced her. Felt fabulous - an extraordinary sensation. Met Peter Eckersley, Baz & Co also Julie & boyfriend. Vicky has many devoted fans, applauding individual jokes.

28th May 1981 Thursday:

Victoria in Bury was in splendid form with a smashing audience, three quarters trendy folk, plus 'with-it' middle-aged - well-groomed hippies & ladies in leather. After the show I was exhausted & felt holy & religious, almost as if I had partaken of a sacred ceremony.

For any of us kids wanting to write and/or perform on the stage our Dad Stan was a great role model. Before the war, he had run his own dance band. After WW2 he continued to play piano with local dance bands as well as at office 'dos' and other events. During his wartime service in the Royal Navy, Stan was based at Devonport near Plymouth where the navy, perhaps surprisingly, found a good use for his talents, putting on shows and editing a sailors' magazine.

Stan was one of a number of writers from the 1930s onwards who wanted to get away from the standard type of plays and films of the day in which the main characters were always upper crust, professional types. Servants and other working people were usually just two-dimensional caricatures and incidental to the story. He strongly believed that working-class life could be shown on stage and screen to be as just as dramatic as upper-class.

In his stories and scripts, Stan was always meticulous in his use of language. Just like Victoria did later, Stan would write and rewrite, often several times. This was good for me: I got sixpence a time for cycling over to Stan's secretary Mrs Partridge for her to do the re-typing. For me, the more the merrier! I still remember her address: 49 Belbeck Street, Bury. On one occasion Stan hovered between 'do the washing up' and 'do the pots', finally at the third attempt deciding on the latter. Our Dad was middle-class, but he fully understood working-class life and language.

Geoff Posner told *The Telegraph*:

> *Before Victoria came along, there was a general feeling in the industry that women - especially northern women - couldn't be funny.*

There's been a lot of debate as to whether Victoria was working-class or middle-class. To me, there's no doubt that us four children had a middle-class upbringing. Although our parents had both come from impoverished backgrounds, they were very much upwardly mobile and their standard of living saw steady improvement over the years. After all, from the age of four Vic was brought up in a big house in the country. Despite that, with her acute observation and retentive memory she was well attuned to working-class ways and created many memorable working-class characters in her work.

Victoria portrayed herself as northern working-class. Certainly she was northern, a Lancashire lass and proud of it. Living in London, married to a London-born entertainer (Geoffrey Durham) and with friends who were all 'in the business', Victoria never became a 'luvvie'. But was she working-class? There have been mixed opinions - even in the same newspaper.

In reality, Victoria was anything but working-class. She had a thoroughly middle-class upbringing. While our Mum and Dad, Nellie (Mape) and Stan Wood, took up their married life after WW2 'living in' with Stan's parents in Manchester before moving on to two rented rooms in a small terraced house in Bury, Lancashire, they were a single-mindedly, upwardly mobile couple determined to give their four children a good start in life, a better standard of living, and the best possible education.

So, Vic was brought up in relative comfort in a great big house out in the country. She was a pupil at Bury Grammar School Girls, an independent, fee-paying school with a fine record of scholastic and sporting achievement. Most of the girls at BGS Girls and its neighbour BGS Boys went on to university - still a rarity in those days - as did I, Victoria and her elder sisters Penny and Rosalind, albeit the latter after attending a different school.

In 2001, *The Telegraph* noted:

> *Like Alan Bennett, Wood speaks to an adoring middle-class constituency in the voice of trans-Pennine northerness. They both have a taste for the precision and exoticism of language and for what it tells us about character. But they're different. Where Bennett's humour is driven by petit-bourgeois standing-on-ceremony, Wood's world view is all about Lancastrian stoicism, about never getting excited or impressed or battered by anything. 'They have a really good way of expressing themselves,' she says, 'It's very unemotional. You'd never say: 'Oh darling, you were marvellous.' People in Lancashire would say: 'Oh that's not bad,' or 'I didn't mind it.'*

Sex after childbirth? It's like full national employment. A lovely idea but I know I'll never see it again in my lifetime.

After Vic's death, Ian Jack wrote in the *Guardian*;

> *What class Wood started out in was this week a moot question. A* Guardian *editorial had her down as working-class: 'A northern, English, working-class Lancastrian and Mancunian female treasure'. But her* Guardian *obituary said she was a middle-class, sophisticated woman whom critics compared to Noël Coward and Alan Bennett'. The second seems nearer the mark. The parental home in Bury, Lancashire, had a piano; her father (was) an insurance salesman, who wrote plays in his spare time; and as Wood was growing up her mother went off to Manchester*

University as a mature student.

When The Observer *interviewer Richard Brooks asked if Wood holidayed in Blackpool, she snapped: 'What do you take me for? We used to go to Vienna'. And they did: the Woods towed their Sprite Musketeer four-berth caravan across Europe for their holidays.*

Now I would also like to claim working-class roots, but they go two generations back. Our mother Nellie Mape certainly was working-class, but from the time she married our Dad Stanley Wood in 1940 she aspired to better things. She became fiercely 'upwardly mobile', cutting herself off from most of her family and making friends of middle-class women in the Ladies Circle and the Costume Society.

I am not criticising Mum for doing this: far from it. It is very much to her credit that she devoted herself to provide a better standard of living and above all the best possible education for her four children. So ours was very definitely a middle-class family.

Although our Dad Stan also had humble origins, his formidable mother Eleanor (my 'posh Nana') was determined that only the best was good enough for her beloved and gifted son Stanley, her only child. Born in Hull but brought up in a big house in Woodhall Spa, Eleanor had been surrounded by servants: she never had to cook, clean or do laundry. Lively and outgoing, she was regularly invited to the nearby 'big house' - Petwood, now a hotel - for dances and to take part in entertainments, and she and her mother were guests at a big society wedding in Westminster Abbey.

Not for nothing I called my posh Nana 'The Duchess'. Her

husband John Wood, our grandfather, was a post office telegraphist, but he came into a bit of money and Eleanor was able to achieve her heart's desire, a 'nice little semi' in the leafy Manchester suburb of Chorlton-cum-Hardy.

In any case, there is no doubt that a great deal of Victoria's humour made mock of the pretensions of the middle-class, particularly the lower middle-class. Freda and Barry (*Let's Do It!*) may well have had working-class parents, but they are without doubt a thoroughly middle-class couple. I would guess that most of Vic's fans have been middle-class, while accepting of course that her humour appealed and indeed still appeals to all classes.

Not so much a complexion - more a doily.

Victoria & Geoff team up on stage. Stan approves: 24th May 1981 Sunday:

We are going to see V (& G) tomorrow at Warrington.

25th May 1981:

Warrington Festival '81. Victoria Wood and the Great Suprendo [sic] in Funny Turns, *Lilford Theatre, Bewsey High School.*

24th November 1981:

To Granada to watch three sketches being shot of Wood & Walters.

31st January 1982:

Television *by Clive James. Already a booming success, Wood and Walters (Granada) should be there for ever...Victoria was a guest critic on* Did You See? *(BBC2).*

14th February 1982:

Last W & W *tonight. Felt quite sad.*

12th January 1986:

Delighted to find mention of Vicky ASOTV *in the* News *of the* World *of all places. 'The funniest thing on the box'. V's show sparkles - gives great uplift to the spirit - particularly the music, which nobody ever mentions.*

5-6th February 1986 Wednesday/Thursday:

Geoff rang up to say Vicks has won an award & she will be on Pebble Mill, *Friday.*

7th February 1986 Friday:

V's Pebble Mill *debut was not bad.*

30th March 1986:

Easter Sunday. V's show was magnificent - a glittering triumph. New show (87%) some super new songs.

13th April 1986 Sunday:

Next Tuesday we go to see V at the Guildhall.

15th April 1986 Tuesday:

Victoria at the Preston Guildhall - a vast, echoing railway station. Vicky was superb but mike was not, variable from boom to lousy buzz.

17th-18th October 1986 Friday/Saturday:

Went to London. Booked in at Scratchwood Motel, then to Shepherd's Bush. Long queue for about 30/45 mins then to Studio 1 - set up for V's rehearsal...V did a warm-up.

Another sister was also entertaining with her songs. In 1985 *The Stage* reported that singer/songwriter Penny Wood was guest for the night on *Lipstick and Lights* with singer Carol Grimes.

In 1989, Vic wrote six half-hour plays for the BBC: *Live with Pam*, Pam played by Walters with Vic as teenage mother Lorraine who dolls up to take Pam's place on a TV show; *Val de Re* sees Vic and Celia Imrie go hill walking; *Mens Sana* takes place on a health farm with Walters as an instructor; *Staying In* features a middle-class dinner party; *The Library* is a repressed librarian love story; *We'd Quite Like to Apologise* is about a delayed airport flight. These were made on film without an audience, but then shown to a live audience to add the laughter.

Vic told me she never, ever read 'crits' of her work. For her, all that mattered was that her audiences were pleased with what she put before them. She was quite happy to accept awards like the BAFTAS, but only on the basis that it was confirmation that she had done was worthwhile. Her attitude on receiving awards was to say 'thank you, I'm glad and happy, but tomorrow I shall put this away and get back to work'. There was no row of BAFTAS on her mantelpiece.

My sister didn't even want to be told of good 'crits'. On one occasion I rang her to tell her about a particularly good review: I said I would send her a copy. 'DON'T!' she snapped,

> *I don't want to know about it. I never, ever read reviews, good or bad.*

Early in her career, Vic had been the subject of some cruel comments from critics, usually about her being overweight.

Her piano playing was criticised by a *New Faces* judge. Her attitude was: what do they know? All that mattered to Vic was her audience.

They expect you to be flighty, and they act like God almighty, because they've got a cock and they can mend a flex.

As Victoria's fame grew, there were no more bad reviews. In retrospect, *The Australian*'s Wendy Harmer wrote:

Wood's breakout performance in the 1981 Secret Policeman's Other Ball Royal Variety performance was with a ditty called I've Had it Up to Here (with men). *She took the stage at the piano in lemon-coloured suit and blonde bob, looking for all the world like the newly married English rose, Princess Diana, and laid waste with this lyric about men: 'They expect you to be flighty, and they act like God almighty, because they've got a cock and they can mend a flex'. She was a champion of the 'little woman'.*

In 2001, a Telegraph review said:

On television, Wood excels at the character-based comedy of dinnerladies *and the award-winning* Pat and Margaret. *On stage she has always returned to the well of her own navel. ('I do try just to be myself on stage, but with better clothes.')*

Except it's not just her navel any more. The last time she toured, the jokes were mostly about bringing up young children. The time before, her subject was pregnancy and birth. Her current preoccupation is the next stage in a woman's journey: middle age, the menopause and, in her case, therapy, an eating disorder and - the showpiece - the emergency hysterectomy she had earlier this year. It is by quite some distance the most graphic she has ever been. She closes the first half of the show by offering to bare her scar, and the second reaches its climax when, in an anecdote about marital sex, she asks her husband if he has reached his own.

The house comes down when she compares her post-op pubic rearrangement to the facial hair of racing tipster John McCririck. This is, in effect, Victoria Wood's private Vagina Monologue. *For straight males in the audience (she boasts of coming second in a gay icon poll), these two hours form a useful guide to the alien creatures they live with. But you can tell from the fusillade of mainly high-pitched shrieks and squeals that Wood has never spoken so directly to women.*

Things have changed since she last toured five years ago. There is a new spikiness, a new confidence. There are some tart references to fellow over-eating north Londoner Vanessa Feltz. Women from Debbie McGee to the Queen are lined up and popped at. There are songs, in the character of Stacey Leanne Paige, slutty star of a docusoap called Luxury Liner, *but Wood no longer plays the piano - 'a totally outmoded instrument'.*

But the main change is that, free from various personal demons, she is also free to use more or less any salty word she chooses. 'I think everything has moved on. If I did what I was doing five years ago it would seem quite mild. I'm just responding to the climate. I'm not saying anything I don't want to say, but it's nice to have a bit more leeway now. I say 'penis': that's about as far as I go. I think I manage to do it in a way that doesn't offend. I'm only interested in what's funny. If I said 'I think that would be a bit scary; people would find that hard to take'. I can vouch for that. I heard her say it and all but fell off my chair.

The show (Albert Hall) was written in haste earlier this year, between the operation and the rearranged try-out dates. The magnificent closing section, in which she describes her efforts to inject some romance into her marriage, was dashed off in an evening once rehearsals had already been and gone. 'I wrote that on the Friday night and did it on the Monday night in Folkestone. It virtually wrote itself'. It reads as a valediction, full of gags about gammy legs, bunions, hernias and love, and takes the place of the routine about old age that Wood would have been doing in twenty years' time.

In 2001 Jasper Rees of *The Telegraph* wrote:

There are about four jokes a minute in Victoria Wood's show. At more than two hours of stage time, that makes, at a conservative guess, 250 laughs a night. Multiply that by the number of performances she will have done by the end of her latest national tour (which began in May and supposedly ends on October 16, though dates are being added all the time), factor in the number of people who will have seen the show (150,000), and it adds up to a lot of laughter. A comedian could easily get hooked.

A white backdrop on the stage of the Oxford Apollo announces the title of the tour: Victoria Wood - At It Again. *And yet when it ends in the spring she actually won't be at it ever again. She's fairly certain that she's giving up live performance. 'I don't want to get totally out of date,' she says. 'Which you just wouldn't know. That's the sad thing.*

I'd be going on doing jokes about Sanatogen. It's best to stop when things are working and not because people are fed up with you'. So when the last laugh of the last show of the last tour has faded after twenty-eight years on the live circuit, Wood will no longer be a stand-up comedian bouncing aerobically around the stage.

I said, Look, I don't expect you to take me out to dinner first, but hello would be nice.

Did you know sex is going out of fashion? It's a little trend I've started.

I saw Vic's stage stand-up show numerous times, doing my best to get to see her perform at least once when she was on her various tours. When Vic was at home she was always extremely busy, always under time constraints. Writing alone took up a huge chunk of her time. Add to that rehearsing, performing, meeting her agent and all the various professionals involved, as well as being 'Mum' to Grace and Henry, seeing Vic on the road was the best chance to have a chat with her either before or after the show. A quick phone call, and she never failed to leave tickets for me at the door.

On stage, Vic would capture her audience in an instant and hold their attention throughout. With her rapid, almost machine-gun like delivery (but always with perfectly timed pauses) and so many gems in every line, the audience just had to pay close attention for fear of missing something. Getting to know her material so well, I spent a lot of the time looking at the audience. To see so many people losing themselves in joy and laughter was a big tonic for me, I can tell you.

In 2001 *The Telegraph's* Jasper Rees wrote:

I wonder over lunch the next day whether she has considered the possibility of withdrawal symptoms when she gives up performing live.

'I'm hoping I'm not addicted, because otherwise I'm going to be miserable when I stop. I'm very aware that that feeling lasts no longer than the end of the show. It is like Chinese food and it's silly to get dependent on it. Although I do love it, it's a very stressful job. I am devoted to comedy and writing jokes and stories, but I wanted to leave myself out of it. I've gone as far as I want to do talking about myself.'

Perhaps it is the right time to stop, with that Tiggerish energy undimmed and the observational wit still as sharp as a tack. 'I've got so many other things I want to do. I just feel another direction looming. I would really like to write some films. I've got things in me that can't necessarily be encapsulated in a stand-up show. You can only follow your instincts and I don't want to drop back down and end up doing little theatres. I'm having a ball, but nobody stays at the top. Very, very few people can keep it going.'

When Victoria died, many of her fans took to social media to express their grief - and their appreciation of all that Vic had done. Stuart McFarlane tweeted:

Saw her stand-up show in Liverpool about fifteen years ago. She was brilliant. At one point she picked out a woman in the audience, pretends to recognize her, and gives a warm greeting in a broad Lancashire accent, 'Ee ello luv how ya doin; are ya still a prostitute?' The woman nods enthusias-

tically and laughs with the rest of audience.

Applecake tweeted:

She was someone I feel I've known throughout my adult life, someone who could be quite biting at times, but never nasty or unfair. She was politically correct before it was even a thing, just by naturally being her. I saw her on stage in the 80s (I think) and she was just so funny. She saw someone eating a chocolate orange in the audience and insisted on having a piece of it - her genius was in making something as simple as that intensely funny, I don't know how.

Isolde2 tweeted:

Her sketch about Ann Widdecombe was done years before Widdecombe was actually on Strictly Come Dancing, making VW eerily prescient about people in public life being desperate to become 'celebrities'.

Clive James wrote in the *Guardian*:

Last night, I watched her yet again in her Brief Encounter spoof, a number that keeps on getting better than ever as Celia Johnson's diamond-cut elocution becomes more and more a thing of the past, like the way the Queen used to speak when she was gist a gel.

CHAPTER SIX

ACORN ANTIQUES

Of all the many memorable characters that Victoria created, the best-known and best-loved is surely that of Mrs Overall, the shuffling, philosophising, pinny-wearing Brummie 'char' who appears at all the wrong moments in Vic's spoof TV sitcom *Acorn Antiques*, originally shown as part *of VWASOTV* 1985-87 and set in the fictitious town of Manchesterford. Vic's unique creation, marvellously portrayed by Julie Walters, Mrs O is the compelling central character in both the spoof soap and Vic's subsequent stage musical.

So strongly did Mrs Overall capture our imaginations that she later became the star of Vic's stage play *Acorn Antiques: The Musical!* which opened at the Theatre Royal in London in 2005. A later version, which Vic produced, has been on tour and is still being played today.

Vic told Richard E Grant:

> One of the highlights of my career, inventing Acorn Antiques. I'm very proud of it. I called it Acorn Antiques because I'd just been working for some people called Acorn Pictures.

> **Well, that certainly SOUNDS like a genuine Picasso. But I would have to see it to be sure.**
>
> **(Miss Babs,** Acorn Antiques**)**

It speaks volumes for Vic's ability to people her productions with the strongest possible cast, and her terrific generosity - almost unique in showbiz - by denying herself the central role and giving the best parts and the best lines to her fellow actors. Victoria could so easily have played Mrs Overall herself and indeed did so superbly on several occasions in her stage production (but only to give Julie Walters a rest). Not only did Vic give Julie the crown jewels in TV's *Acorn Antiques* as Mrs Overall, she gave herself the minor role of co-owner Berta, far less prominent even than Celia Imrie's flakey shop owner/manager Miss Babs. The ever-reliable Duncan Preston played Miss Babs' love interest Mr Clifford, and Kenny Ireland was the simple-minded handyman Derek.

So strong a character was Mrs Overall that the fictitious actress and 'national treasure' who 'played' her, Bo Beaumont had a spin-off life of her own. In *Victoria Wood's Midlife Christmas* (2009) Walters plays Beaumont who is desperate to rebuild her career after being sacked from the soap *Acorn Antiques*.

The enduring charm of *Acorn Antiques* in *VWASOTV* is Vic's pure genius of taking the things that go wrong with a cheaply produced, hackneyed TV sitcom with banal lines delivered by struggling actors to the absolute limit. Its ridiculosities are so absurd they are almost beyond parody, and all the more funny because of that. We laugh and laugh again and again at the wonky sets, the useless props, the utterly stupid and unbelievable storylines (which are introduced incongruously and at random before being abruptly abandoned), actors missing their cues or entering too early, the furious ad-libbing, slowly moving in or out of shot, and the chaotic credits which always included 'Victoria Woods' - I could go on.

Memorably, Clive James wrote:

> *Towering above everything (or rather creeping round behind) is the ubiquitous presence of Mrs Overall, dispensing coffee and platitudes at every turn'. Another critic described Mrs Overall as being like Amy Turtle, the* Crossroads *dogsbody.*

Vic said she always wanted to write a sitcom (*dinnerladies*) and she always wanted to write a stage musical. This she did with *Acorn Antiques*. The preview on January 31st 2005 had mixed reviews, but the show's run from February 9th to May 21st was popular with the public. With Vic replacing Sir Trevor Nunn as director, the show had a seven-month tour of twenty-four cities, starting at Salford December 2006.

Sometimes I think that being widowed is God's way of telling you to come off the pill.

(Mrs Overall, Acorn Antiques)

Acorn Antiques: The Musical! was (and is) a great joy. Here was Vic's own creation on the London stage. My wife Frances and I went to see it three times. We had originally intended to go twice, once with Victoria in the lead role as Mrs Overall, and once with Julie Walters who was billed as the main star. Prosaically, Vic realised that eight shows a week might be too much for her friend Julie. So Vic took over the role of Mrs O on Mondays and for Saturday matinees. Quipping as always, Vic said:

Julie plays the main role as Mrs Overall, but I take over on bingo nights.

So why three times? Well, we wanted to see both Vic and Julie as Mrs O. First we went to see Vic, who was of course terrific (what else could she be?). We took my granddaughter Emily Wood, aged eleven at the time. Emily has always wanted to be an actor and had shown her desire to perform from the age of three when she recruited me and my wife as supporting actors as she played Cinderella, Esmerelda etc in our living room. Previously we had taken Em to a number of West End shows which she adored.

I mention this because Emily later became a stand-up comic herself, appearing at the Edinburgh Fringe in 2012 (prior to my own modest debut the following year), and is now an up-and-coming actor, model and presenter: look her up. Needless to say, Emily was entranced with Victoria's performance and even more so when we took her backstage to meet her famous great-aunt. Vic signed her programme which Emily held tightly in her hand throughout our train journey back to the North East.

Just as Victoria Wood was enthused and motivated by seeing Joyce Grenfell on stage and meeting her afterwards, so I believe that seeing Victoria on stage and meeting her afterwards has similarly inspired Emily Wood - but as a doting brother and grandfather, I would say that, wouldn't I?

Then we booked to see Julie Walters as Mrs O. Now there's a strict rule in the theatre, that if a star is unable to appear at one particular performance, the audience must be informed before the show. They then have the choice of watching the show with an understudy in that role, or getting their money back.

When we arrived at the Theatre Royal to see Julie, there was this notice: 'We regret to inform patrons that Julie Walters will not be appearing tonight as she is unwell. The role of Mrs Overall will be taken by Victoria Wood. ANY PATRONS WHO DO NOT WISH TO SEE THE SHOW TONIGHT SHOULD APPLY TO THE BOX OFFICE FOR ALTERNATIVE TICKETS OR THEIR MONEY BACK' (my capitals).

So we saw Vic as Mrs O on stage a second time. Later, I said jokingly to Vic: 'how ridiculous! Surely no-one would miss the chance to see you play Mrs Overall?' To my surprise, Vic replied:

'Don't you believe it. I'm told there were thirty-forty people who did ask for their money back!' They couldn't all be Julie's relatives, surely?

We did get to see Julie Walters as Mrs O at a later date. She was, of course, superb. Don't ask me to choose which of these two wonderful actors was the better in that role, although I will say that while I admired Vic both as a comedy and as a dramatic actor, that Julie has the greater range and has played a number of parts that just would not suit Vic. She can play anything!

Never mind. Bingo Tuesday (Mrs Overall, on losing her husband).

During her years of struggle, Victoria was determined to succeed with her own unique brand of humour. There was to be no compromise, no 'man walks into a bar' gag-telling, Bob Monkhouse style. So when Vic made it to the top of her profession, she knew precisely what was funny and what was not. Woe betide anyone, regardless of their position or importance, who tried to tell her what comedy was.

When a BBC executive made an ill-judged attempt to guide Victoria, she hit back:

What's your qualification for telling me what's funny? Don't tell me funny - I know what's funny. That's why I'm on television and you're not.

As if brilliant writing, comedy and acting were not enough to ensure the finished product was what she wanted to present to the public, Victoria added another essential element very much of her own: control. Vic realised, or decided (or perhaps a combination of both) that to get the best results and to achieve her vision, she would have to have control of the whole process. In this she was absolutely determined and single-minded - implacably so.

Producer Geoff Posner told *The Telegraph*:

I learned to respect her particular way of writing, and to see it as my job simply to show it in the best possible way - a lesson that would stay with me in all the programmes I would go on to make, from French and Saunders *to* Little Britain. *There's a lot of interference working in television nowadays, but Vic couldn't be interfered with; it would defeat the whole purpose of what she was doing, and that's why it's so sad she has left us.*

Long-term co-star Duncan Preston:

She (Victoria) was very demanding to work for and wanted it right. She knew what was right and what was wrong. She had an inbuilt knack of seeing comedy in people and writing it. The famous Two Soups *sketch came about while she was having a cuppa in Morecambe. Something about the waitress in the local café inspired her and Victoria wrote a sketch about it.*

Vic admitted that she was a control freak, albeit 'a control freak but quite jolly with it'. That was the only way she could be certain what appeared before the public, whether on stage, on radio, film or TV, would be exactly as she wished it to be. She knew exactly what she wanted, and she would brook no opposition or interference in how she achieved that. But Vic was good, very, very good, and wisely her colleagues went along with her sometimes demanding ways.

Add to that, Vic was concerned about her public image: not for any reasons of vanity or self-aggrandisement (she was one of the least egotistic stars I have ever met) but because she knew that her image, her fame, was a massive plus for her in being able to do what she wanted to do the way she wanted it, and enabled her to move from one field of endeavour to another. Sometimes 'image' and 'control' were in conflict.

Vic told me more than once that, almost from the very start, she had worked hard to protect her public image. A film clip showing her bluntly pointing out the deficiencies of an actor or any of the crew would have damaged her public persona as a much-loved performer whose comedy was revealing but never cruel. Only once did her iron grip slip, albeit just for a few seconds.

Sometimes Victoria would allow the television cameras into rehearsals to record a 'fly on the wall' documentary. The completed films, as transmitted, show a dedicated group of actors happily working together, as indeed was the case - most of the time. That the occasional storm clouds were not shown is due to Victoria's determination and to her ability to exercise complete editorial control. Anything she disapproved of had to be cut.

Victoria was rehearsing her musical play *That Day We Sang* and was being filmed for a TV documentary. She was doing a read-though with the cast when she lost her place. 'Oh dear, I've lost my place - I've turned over two pages together!' she chortled. The other actors dutifully joined in the laughter, during which one is heard to say

that's not what she says when WE do it!

Geoff Posner told *The Telegraph*:

> *Vic had a very clear vision of what she wanted. Even when she was performing in a sketch herself, she would keep an eye on the whole scene - what she and everybody else was doing.*

Vic's outbursts were rare, especially as over the years she gathered around her a group of people she respected and with whom she was happy to work. With her ever-flowing spring of comedy genius constantly bubbling through, working with Vic was for the most part a great joy, constantly punctuated with laughter.

> **Gainsborough's Blue Boy? Yes, I think we have that in mauve.** **(Miss Babs)**

Victoria was always happy to make fun of other television productions. Her 2009 Christmas Show included *Lark Pies to Candlestickford*, a take-off of *Lark Rise to Candleford*, *Little Dorrit* and *Cranford*. The actors are shown frozen in their starting positions before 'Action' is called, something I can attest to from my occasional outings as a TV/film extra.

The language in *Candlestickford* mimics its originals, but with pies and potatoes incongruously replacing more serious subjects. Vic plays the feisty, buxom postmistress with great relish, voicing numerous sexual innuendos so convincingly they never descend to *Carry On* type smut. There are nods to modernity, for example, a group of (Georgian) teenage girls screaming as they are driven through a water splash in a horse-drawn cart. A quick-draw sketch artist records the moment à la modern theme park roller-coaster rides.

Vic adds another chapter to her funny but incisive view of

'women's problems' with the *Midlife Olympics from Brentford, Middlesex*. One of the female competitors is drug-tested for sugar, perhaps an echo of Vic's own battles. It was the realisation that she was addicted to sugar that gave her the key to reducing her weight.

Vic always said that she enjoyed acting more than writing, which could be a chore. But it got easier as time went on. In 2009 Victoria told the *Mail*'s Frances Hardy:

> *I wrote* Talent *in longhand in our flat in Morecambe at night after the telly had closed down; there was no 24-hour viewing in those days. I'd go to bed in the day and Geoff would type up what I'd written, which really was a sign of devotion because he couldn't actually type.*

And in 2011 Victoria told Chrissy Iley of *The Telegraph*:

> *I like writing a lot more than I used to. I used to find it scary but now I've got used to it once it gets going. I used to find it hard to start. Fear of the blank page. The first thing you write down won't bear any relation to what's in your head and that's always disappointing.*

Stan recorded his own successes, as well as his daughter's:

19th July 1978 Wednesday:

> *Super letter from Tony Cliff of Leeds who has sent* Summer of '28 *to the man who edits* Afternoon Theatre.

10th October 1978 Sunday:

> *Great trip today. Took Victoria & Geoff & all their gear from Sheffield in two hours travelling 120 miles. On Sat we checked in at the Grosvenor Hotel, first rate. Victoria's* Talent *a stage musical is first rate, magnificent, funny, a*

good musical satire on talent contests, songs super. Granada wants to buy it & no wonder.

It was while Victoria was writing sketches for the revue *In at the Death* at London's Bush Theatre, that David Leland, then director at the Crucible theatre, Sheffield, invited her to write a play for its 1978 new season. This was Vic's first play *Talent*, which she wrote specifically for her friend Julie Walters. Two girls are getting ready backstage for a talent show when they realise the contest is rigged. Paul Allen wrote in the *Guardian*:

It incorporated a wealth of human disillusion and more comic one-liners than is altogether fair in a sad, sad story. Its problem, he wrote, *was that it was sometimes too knicker-wettingly funny.*

Ironically, Julie was not available to appear as her namesake in the original stage production of *Talent,* but she took over the role that was always meant for her in the TV version which not only showed Julie's great talent as a comic actress, but also cemented the on-screen relationship of her and Victoria which brought us so many memorable moments in the years to come. It was a friendship and a collaboration made in heaven!

Ante-natal classes are run by liars. When you're having a baby for the first time what you really need to know is, 'what's it going to be like?' And they won't tell you.

Stan's Journal: 13-14th January 1980 *Still in a state of euphoria.* April 1980 Cutting from Manufacturers Life Insurance staff magazine: *Stanley Wood, 30 years. Officially retired in 1977, he is still writing a substantial amount of business. Back home in Manchester, Stanley was until quite recently the impresario of our Branch functions, scripting and producing entertainments ranging from Pantomime and Broadway Hits to Old Time Music Halls.*

9th January 1981:

> Wood & Walters *was marvellous Vicky's next 75-min play will not include her.*

7th August 1981:

Wife called, heard mention of Victoria's new play on Granada on Sunday (*Happy Since I Met You*, third in series). Lady critic was most enthusiastic about it, saying it was her best yet. This was the pilot programme. There were seven episodes of *Wood & Walters* in 1982.

The Happiest of Birthdays
  I wish you Dearest Wife;
For you have brought sweet melody.
And sunshine to my life.
As we travel on together.
  Beneath a cloudless sky.
My love for you grows stronger,
With each year that passes by.
Wood

July 1 1993

They say that elderly people may need a message repeating more than once. This card is to convey my opinion of you, my dear husband, on your birthday, and always.

Helen

It always is a pleasure
At this time of year
To send a Birthday message
That's hearty and sincere!

MANY HAPPY RETURNS

All My Love
  for ever.
Wood xxx

28 'Wood' was Nellie's pet name for her husband Stan; theirs was a lifelong romance, despite regular rows

Dear Father.
  Here are the photos

Did you get a nice retiring present? We are having our garden done which means both the front and back doors have to be open all day to let

various boys through with wheelbarrows of things – its freezing. And now they have just started cutting York stone with an electric saw so noisy as well.

  lots of love
  Vicky.

29 Victoria was very close to her doting Dad

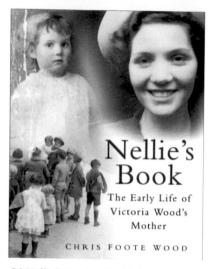

31 Bury Grammar School Boys, now taken over by BGS Girls with the Boys moving into a new building

30 Nellie's Book - Chris's biography of his mother 2006. Victoria wrote the foreword. For the last 40 years of her life, Nellie refused to speak to her son Chris and forbade him to visit. To this day, nobody knows why, and Nellie never gave any reason

Kenneth McPherson

Victoria Wood

Dear M —

Don't show this to Father. Can you give him his card on his birthday, please —

I might forget to post it on the right day.

And — I have bought him a piano — it will beat Forsyth Bros

in Deansgate in about 10 days.

I've paid for the delivery — you can either phone them and arrange for it to be delivered or just take Father to the shop — it's up to you.

It is a YAMAHA C108 UPRIGHT – black. Their phone no. is 834·3281, and they know about it being a surprise.

love Vicky.

32 Victoria buys a new piano for her Dad's birthday, wants to keep it a secret

'TICKLING MY IVORIES' is an evening of singing, talking, sketches, standing up, sitting down again, and possibly one card trick.

It is available for theatres, community centres, arts festivals and cabaret.

PLEASE SEND ALL ENQUIRIES TO:

VICTORIA WOOD
12 OXFORD STREET
MORECAMBE
LANCS.
LA4 5JF

(0524) 417092 24-hour answering service.

33 Tickling My Ivories - *Victoria's early self-promoted solo stage show*

34 Success for the 'Queen of Comedy' - on the front page of the Radio Times *(November 1986),* TV Quick *(November 1991),* You Magazine *(June 1998)*

35 Make People Matter, 1987 - Victoria never openly supported
any political party, but she felt strongly about social issues

36 Victoria makes a
rare appearance on
a TV quiz show, QI
2013

37 Manchester's Victoria Station was renamed Victoria Wood Station,
just for one hour in 2016

38 Chris and his second wife Frances on Brighton Palace Pier, 2008. They were together for 40 years before Frances died of cancer in 2013 aged 68

39 Proud day: Frances awarded the OBE in the 1992 New Year's Honours for her many years of full-time, unpaid voluntary service. This well-earned honour was widely welcomed

40 Chris on stage at The Sage, Gateshead 2012

41 Chris as the new James Bond - not!

42 Victoria and her brother Chris (13 years older) were not close, but they cared for each other

43 Chris takes granddaughter Emily Wood to see *Victoria* play Mrs Overall in her stage musical Acorn Antiques *at the Theatre Royal in London's Haymarket, February 2005. Emily had been stage-struck from the age of three*

44 Emily Wood makes her debut with her solo stand-up comedy show at the Edinburgh Festival Fringe 2013. Emily is now an actor, model and presenter

45 Chris made his Edinburgh Fringe debut in 2014 with his one-man show The Genius of Charles Dickens

*46 Victoria as Chris most fondly remembers her,
relaxing at their annual family gatherings*

*47 Siblings, in birth order
(l-r) Chris, Penelope, Rosalind and Victoria (Skipton c. 2000)*

All photographs in this section are the property of the Author

CHAPTER SEVEN

dinnerladies

What was it like working with the multi-talented, driven Victoria Wood? Almost everyone who has worked with her will tell you it is stimulating, enjoyable, satisfying - and very, very hard. Victoria demanded the highest standards of creative performance from herself, and she expected nothing less from everybody else.

Often combining the roles of writer, actor, producer and director, Victoria had a clear vision not only of the finished product, but how it was to be achieved. She would admonish anyone falling short in clear and simple language. Always direct, Victoria was never a 'luvvie' in any sense of the word. Finding it necessary to live in London due to her work, and wanting to spend as much time as she could with her two children, Victoria remained a down-to-earth northern girl, blunt and to the point.

Victoria's great strength was to be able to write compelling roles and dialogue for herself and her fellow actors. Despite writing every word for her shows, she was never the only star. Right from the start with her first television sketch show with her lifelong friend and co-star Julie Walters, Vic insisted that there had to be equal billing, hence the title *Wood and Walters*. Even with *Victoria Wood: As Seen On TV* it was a cast of actors, with everyone having their individual features, although Vic opens with a great piece of stand-up.

Acorn Antiques, both as part of *VWASOTV* and on stage, and *dinnerladies* were most decidedly ensemble pieces, never a star vehicle.

Vic's long-time friend and actor Duncan Preston told the *Sun*:

> Me, Julie Walters, Celia Imrie and Susie Blake were Victoria's inner circle. She trusted us and we became a small rep company in our own right. But Victoria wrote for the girls, really.

The *Mirror*'s Carole Malone wrote:

> *Victoria Wood was content to let other people be the 'stars' even though many would never have been stars without her genius. She wrote her best lines for others.*

Producer Geoff Posner told *The Telegraph*:

> *Victoria wrote every single word of all the projects we did together: she was so generous in giving other actors great sketches to be in that I had to coax her into appearing in them herself.*

> **What were they called...them things like cucumbers ...suffragettes.'** (***Twinkle***, dinnerladies)

Victoria always wanted to write a sitcom, and she succeeded in spades with *dinnerladies*. This much-loved series, set in a works canteen, is probably the best example of Vic's ability to write an 'ensemble piece', in which she was just one of a cast of characters, each with his/her own personality.

Vic wrote the first series of her TV sitcom *dinnerladies* in 1998. Based in a workplace canteen, Victoria plays head cook Bren, Walters her embarrassing, eccentric mother Petula, Celia Imrie the harassed supervisor Philippa, Duncan Preston the handyman Stan, with Andrew Dunn as Vic's love interest Tony, the canteen supervisor. The gang of 'dinner ladies' included Maxine Peake (Twinkle), Shobna Gulati (Anita), Anne Reid (Jean) and Thelma Barlow (Dolly). Dora Bryan and Thora Hird each made a single appearance.

> ***Advice for wives: Leave the top button of your pyjamas undone, set your balaclava at a jaunty angle, and if he wants to make love, put that book down!***

To research for *dinnerladies*, in March 1997 Vic got first-hand experience working on the early morning canteen shift at the James Halstead factory in Whitefield, Manchester. One of the Halstead brands is Polyflor vinyl flooring. This very much brings to mind a line from Vic's best-know song, *The Ballad of Barry and Freda*: (*I Can't Do It!*) *Let me read this catalogue on vinyl flooring!* which had been written some years earlier. Did Vic choose Halsteads for that reason, I wonder?

The *dinnerladies* sitcom was co-produced by Vic's own company *Good Fun* and Geoff Posner's company *Pozzitive*. The first series was broadcast in 1998, the second series the following year. Vic confessed to me that the second series of *dinnerladies* was the only project she had ever undertaken where she had not written everything in advance. For the first series, she did her 'usual', writing ten episodes and dropping four as not up to standard before any filming was started. It was not so for the second series, which she did only with the greatest reluctance.

> *I definitely didn't want to do a second series,* she told me, *but I was under so much pressure I agreed to do it before I had written all the episodes, which is not the way I like to work. It wasn't easy having to write the later episodes at the same time as we were filming the early ones. It was extremely stressful and I told myself I would never do that again.*

She didn't. For Vic, preparation was all important.

> **The first day I met my producer, she said, 'I'm a radical feminist lesbian'. I thought what would the Queen Mum do? So I just smiled and said, 'We shall have fog by tea-time.'**
> (Kitty)

A number of the cast of *dinnerladies* and *Acorn Antiques* have remarked about Victoria's habit of rewriting scenes overnight after the first rehearsal, distributing the revised version the next day. 'We were constantly re-learning our lines,' says veteran actress Anne Reid. Vic admitted:

> I'd always want to change things, so I'd work through the night to make sure it was as I wanted it.

Anne Reid told Steve Mills of the Northants Post:

> I was just devastated to hear the news [of Vic's death] because for me, she will always be alive, she's someone like Eric Morecambe who to me is always just around the corner. She was also the sort of person who recognised that I could do comedy and opened that door up for me so I'll always be grateful. I hadn't done much comedy before except little bits with Benny Hill.

Anne went on:

> dinnerladies *was hard work, especially at the time as there was a lot of rewrites, right up to the wire with that, sometimes even two hours before the recording. But it was very rewarding.*

Victoria put even more effort than usual into *dinnerladies*. For long periods she survived on only four hours' sleep. This was due in large measure to her own determination to get everything, if not exactly right, at least as good as she could make it. That involved rewrites - lots of them.

Victoria's dedication to getting everything just right, no matter how long it took, was confirmed by producer Geoff Posner who told *The Telegraph*:

When we made dinnerladies, *she wrote ten episodes for the first series, throwing four away simply because they weren't good enough. We'd shoot each episode twice in front of an audience: once, on a Friday night.*

Then, the next morning Vic would come around and watch the recording and she would constantly say 'could this be better? Is this line right? What can I rewrite? She'd spend a couple of hours rewriting and teaching the cast the new lines, and then we'd record the (nearly) same show again the next evening. The pressure on her must have been enormous, but she seemed to thrive on it.

(Telegraph 24.04.16)

In 2011 *The Telegraph*'s Chrissy Iley quoted Victoria:

When you do a BBC sitcom it starts on a Monday and you record on a Friday so it's all very pushed. I'd always want to change things so I'd work through the night to make sure it was as I wanted it.

'Excuse me, this tuna and sweetcorn, it's all mixed up. What I really wanted was tuna and sweetcorn separately.' Twinkle: 'We don't do tuna and sweetcorn. We only do tuna 'n sweetcorn.'

Victoria's constant rewrites put a strain on the cast and crew as well as onto Vic herself. To produce her shows - and remember Victoria was not only writing the dialogue and stage directions, she was also writing the songs and music - Vic would spend weeks and months writing, writing and writing. Always the perfectionist, Vic would write, rewrite and rewrite again until she felt something was exactly right.

The public pay to see what we do, and it's only right that we should make it as good as it possibly can be, she said.

For her one-woman stand-up shows, Vic would 'road test' her material piece by piece, doing twenty minute spots at various 'pub theatres' - pubs with small stages, of which there are many in London - and altering her scripts and lyrics depending on audience reaction. It was a long and painful process. With her machine-gun like delivery, and at least one unique gem in every line, her two-hour show required a huge amount of material - all original. Only when every element, one-liners, stories and songs, were as near perfect as Vic could make them, would she take her show on the road.

Husband Geoff was very much a 'hands-on' Dad and would hold the fort while Vic was creating her masterpieces, a slow, lengthy and painful process.

Vic would lock herself in her study for weeks on end, he told me, *all you would hear were curses and paper being ripped out of the typewriter. But it was all worth it.*

Making, serving and drinking tea was a regular theme in Vic's comedy, as indeed it was in her own life. In *dinnerladies*, Victoria's character Bren was always suggesting a brew, so it was no surprise to see the 2013 BBC TV documentary, *Victoria Wood's Nice Cup Of Tea.*

As Victoria and Morrisey, vocalist of indie rock band *The Smiths*, discussed the merits of a good old cuppa, it was Morrisey, a big fan of Victoria, who tried a joke.

This is just a beanie - this is what the skateboarding kids wear, he said, as he looked at the tea cosy Vic was offering.

Nice Cup of Tea was a two-part special for the BBC. As the

Beeb put it: 'Comedy legend Victoria Wood travels the globe to explore Britain's love affair with tea in a two part special on the little plant that changed the world.

There was archive footage of June Brown as Dot Cotton, Jean Alexander as Hilda Ogden, Julie Walters as Mrs Overall, Winston Churchill and Gracie Fields. Directed by John Moulson and written by Vic (who else?). Victoria interviewed Graham Norton, *Dr Who* star Matt Smith and Morrisey.

Always wanting to keep her private life private, and ever mindful of maintaining her public image as a working-class northerner, Victoria was very cautious about revealing her home life and would not appear in programmes like *Who do you think you are?* When her childhood home Birtle Edge House was shown on TV, the cameras did not reveal its full extent. I'm sure that was Vic's influence at work.

When you're in the middle of having a baby, it's a bit like watching two very inefficient removal men, trying to get a very large sofa through a very small doorway. Only in this case you can't say, 'Oh sod it, bring it through the French windows.

By the time Victoria, the youngest of us four children, came along in 1953, the Wood family had moved on from their first real home, a small semi, to a large end of terraced house, both in Bury. When Vic was four and I was sixteen, we all moved into Birtle Edge House, Nellie and Stan's 'dream home'. The sheer size of Birtle Edge meant that every member of the family, including each of us four children, could have his/her own large bedroom. No more sharing! The parents each had their individual dressing room: also Stan his study and Nellie her sewing room. There was a large entrance hall, big enough to hold a dance, with its grand piano.

Each of us four children was encouraged to do his or her 'own thing', and we were given a huge amount of individual freedom. Being bright, intelligent kids, we made the most of it, and we enjoyed being left to our own devices. I don't recall the 'aged parents' every asking me where I was going when I went out (which was almost every evening). Victoria has said that if she had gone missing, it would have been two or three days before anyone noticed.

The age gap between each of us kids, and Vic being naturally shy and unsure of what she wanted to do (apart from music), and the isolated position of our home, all added to her acute loneliness. There was no question of us being physically neglected. We were always well fed and clothed, we had pocket money, holidays and weekly family day trips, but there was little contact with our parents other than at mealtimes. Dad and I did talk quite often, but Mum was reticent. At Birtle, she never ate with us, as she always seemed to be dieting.

A man is designed to walk three miles in the rain to phone for help when the car breaks down, and a woman is designed to say, 'You took your time' when he comes back dripping wet.

Whether due to her upbringing or her early years living on the breadline, 'eating mince out of a tin', Vic was always careful with money and in fact lived a very abstemious life. She became a vegetarian, didn't smoke or drink, kept herself fit and spent very little on clothes or on herself in general. To me, her main expenditure was on her children. Both went to very good schools which no doubt cost plenty. Vic kept a holiday home near Skipton in Yorkshire and there were other family holidays. She had her own staff, of course, both to support her professional work and to help look after the children.

Having had a useless manager for three years at the start of her career, in later years Vic made sure she maximised her earnings. Not only did she write all her own material, including songs and lyrics, for her shows, and play in them, she often doubled up as producer and/or director, no doubt earning an extra crust. When she was about to complete a stand-up tour, the show would be filmed and released on DVD made by her own company. Vic bonded with Phil McIntyre who became her long-term agent and friend and was executive producer on *dinnerladies*, for example.

Once she had agreed to an interview, Victoria could show great patience and understanding, as in her encounter with the *Mirror*'s Fiona Phillips in the late 90s. To her horror, Phillips found that the recorded interview she had made with Victoria was unusable, and it was with great trepidation that she asked if Vic could do it again. She wrote:

I needn't have worried because, following panic-stricken, apologetic, grovelling phone calls, there came a sight I'll never forget - Victoria Wood arriving back where we'd left off, a 'don't worry, these things happen' on her lips, a smile on her face, and off we went and did it all over again.

CHAPTER EIGHT

HOUSEWIFE, 49

I have always maintained that comics make good actors. After all, it's their job to stand on stage and pretend to be someone else. Even if that 'someone else' is mainly based on their own persona, it's still an artificial concept that has to be reproduced every time they appear on stage or in front of the camera. Think of Russ Abbott, Billy Connelly, Mike Reid, Bill Maynard, Dave King - all successful comics and actors - and the doyen of them all, Peter Sellers. *Little Britain* stars David Walliams and Matt Lucas have both shone as actors. So it was no surprise to me when Vic emerged as an actor, and a very good one at that.

I told Vic more than once that she should do more acting, but of course there were so many other things she wanted to do, writing, producing and directing, that she simply did not have the time. She told Chrissy Iley of *The Telegraph*:

> *Acting is not my favourite thing. I don't like wearing costumes and wigs. I suppose you can do it without costumes and wigs, but then I'd just be playing myself and there wouldn't be any point.*

Vic was drawn first to music. Playing the piano on her own but in front of an imaginary audience, at the end of a number she would turn and bow. As a teenager, Vic turned to acting. She performed on stage with the Rochdale Youth Workshop, and acted in a school play at Bury Grammar School Girls.

Victoria first set out to be an actress. She was perfectly capable of playing any role, but was inevitably overlooked by directors who much preferred to cast 'tall willowy blondes' in female parts. Not only that, Vic auditioned in vain with theatre companies and stage schools: not one would take her. Vic appeared in only one school play at Bury Grammar School Girls, according to her 'because I didn't do my homework'. She took the part of Autolycus in Shakespeare's *The Winter's Tale*. She tried in vain to get into acting school but completed a drama degree at Birmingham University.

From aged fifteen to eighteen Vic found a home (and also a boyfriend) in the Rochdale Youth Theatre Workshop. Here she found fulfilment, acting and writing sketches. She then set out to be an actress. Having failed to get into drama school, Vic settled instead for a drama degree course at Birmingham University. Even there she was not encouraged to act on stage, her tutors suggesting she would be better advised to be stage manager.

In my day we didn't have sex education, we just picked up what we could off the television.

Stan noted his daughter's acting career in his daily Journal: 19-20 September 1970:

Rochdale Theatre Workshop: V quite good but not supported. No director or producer. David Morton's Blue Devil was excellent. V was wonderful as school teacher and as a conductor.

3rd January 1971 Sunday:

Vicky and Bob in Dr Faustus. Their scenes were all right.

13th January 1971:

Vicky had just interview and audition (did Caliban the monster) at Polytechnic School of Music and Drama, All Saints.

17th February 1971 Wednesday:

Vicky came back from London. Had quite a good interview but she speaks badly & needs audio dentology or teeth correction.

1st April 1971:

> *Vicky offered provisional place @ Birmingham University subject to 2 Bs & 1 C.*

24th June 1971 Thursday:

> *Did I record that Vicky is now a paid actress with the Summer Co., basic rate being £6 a week.*

17th July 1971:

> *V is in Bo'ness. Made a mistake with the theatre. It is not in Bo'ness but Keswick.*

So Vic did get a summer job acting, but it didn't lead anywhere. Perhaps we should be grateful that Vic did not get more acting work in her early years: we might have been denied the comedy and her wonderful writing.

Told by her tutors at university to forget acting and be a stage manager, as she was in 1973 with the Department of Drama and Theatre Arts presentation *The Way of the World*, Vic finally took her revenge. Given the job of playing the piano as the audience left at the end of the play, Victoria told them to stay. She sang and played a song she had written about being overlooked for a part in the play!

Fellow drama student and later producer and theatre director Jude Kelly recalled:

> *Victoria was never going to be cast as the classic female lead, or indeed a conventional anything. She wasn't svelte in any way, so although she wanted to try her hand at playing leads - and did in one Greek drama - she didn't fit in with the methods of the (mostly male) tutors of the day. I don't think she felt she could flower in that context. Yet her*

stagecraft was superb: without drawing attention to herself, Victoria's performances were outstanding.

When I moved into a tiny terraced house in Birmingham owned by the writer Fidelis Morgan, and where Victoria lived, in my first year of university in 1972, I was immediately taken with her now-familiar ironic scepticism about people's behaviour. Victoria, who was in the year above me, could pinpoint and puncture any kind of hypocrisy or pumped-up-ness with humour. She had us crying with laughter from the beginning, yet could be shy to the point of reclusiveness, never wanting to be the life and soul of the party. With her friends and on a one-to-one basis, she was unbelievably funny, entertaining and thoughtful. But I remember being intimidated by her fierce cleverness too.

In her third year she moved into her own flat in Edgbaston with her piano, composing songs. You'd go around, listen to her work and I can recall thinking, I am watching the next Noël Coward or Joyce Grenfell. I don't think she had that sense of herself at the time, but I did. It was that quality of purpose mixed with vulnerability. Victoria was single minded, seeing herself as a soloist and the author of her own material.

Meanwhile, she was quite happy to support her friends in their performances. I used to sing and she suggested I went for a job in a jazz club, helping me prepare and acting as my accompanist at the audition. She did have a devilish side too. Victoria wasn't wholesome or goody-goody, but capable of being quite naughty, and utterly human.

Victoria starred in the first three plays she wrote for Granada, *Talent, Nearly a Happy Ending*, and *Happy Since I Met You*. In 1989 Vic wrote and starred in six short plays for the BBC: *Mens Sana in Thingummy Doodah, The Library, We Would Quite Like to Apologise, Over to Pam, Val de Ree*, and *Staying In*. *Pat and Margaret* came in 1994, and in 2005 Vic played Mrs Overall in her musical stage play *Acorn Antiques: The Musical!* twice a week to give regular Mrs O (Julie Walters) a rest. Then came *Housewife, 49* in 2006. On Boxing Day 2007 Vic appeared as 'Nana' in Granada's adaption of the Noel Streatfeild novel *Ballet Shoes*.

A minor operation is one performed on somebody else.

In 1994 Victoria wrote the script for the BBC Screen One TV film *Pat and Margaret,* directed by Gavin Millar. It's the story of two sisters, one a glamorous US soap star, the other a mousey, overweight waitress at a motorway service station, who are reunited after twenty-seven years in a *Surprise, Surprise* type TV show. Interviewed by the *Guardian*'s Stuart Jeffries, Victoria admitted:

> that there was more than a little of Pat in her, the woman so determined to get on there's no room for anything else,

but she wrote that role for Walters and instead played disappointed Margaret herself.

Of *Pat and Margaret*, Vic said: 'it was both of me. It was that battle between the one who can never get on, a sort of impotent person, and the one who's determined to get on there's no room for anything else'. Originally titled *Sisters*, Vic sold the script to LWT who liked it but didn't take it forward. Vic bought back the rights and sold them to BBC for less, but the Beeb made the film which was transmitted on Screen One on September 11th 1994:

Margaret's all the people who don't have a voice and don't have any way of getting themselves up the ladder,

Vic reflected. But she was also playing Margaret as homage to the woman she could have been.

If I'm honest there is part of me that feels, or rather felt, very vulnerable and patronised and this is my way of showing that side of myself.

The two women meet on the TV show, hosted by the excruciatingly 'sincere' Maeve, played to the hilt by Anne Reid whose aside 'this is the best one yet' when *Pat and Margaret* have an awkward embrace is a perfect embellishment.

Victoria kindly wrote the foreword to the book I wrote about our mother's early life, *Nellie's Book* (2006). Nellie didn't keep a diary as such, but she did write down her reminisces in notebooks and on scraps of paper. I was able to put these together to construct Mum's story. Nellie had asked Stan to put her biography together, but he never did - typical of a talented guy who had ten new ideas every day of which very few were ever brought to fruition. I decided to complete the task my father hadn't even started.

I just wonder if this gave Vic the idea of making a drama from a diary, but I wouldn't dream of taking any credit away from my talented and resourceful sister. *Nella Last's Diary*, taken from what she wrote on a daily basis for Mass-Observation in WW2, was published in 1981. Following the success of *Housewife, 49* in 2006, a second edition of Nella's diaries was published.

Of all the things Victoria has done, outside of her comedy, I think the best she has ever done is to play the lead role in the TV film *Housewife, 49* to perfection. Of all the awards she has received, the BAFTA Vic got for 'best actress' (and remember she also got the BAFTA for best writer for it as well) is what stands out the most for me.

Nella Last was aged forty-nine when she started putting her thoughts and feelings on paper for Mass-Observation in September 1939. At first glance this was simply an 'ordinary' housewife coping with wartime conditions. Vic's great insight was to bring this 'ordinary' woman to life and to show her strengths and weaknesses, difficulties and achievements, in three-dimensional technicolour. To do this so superbly as writer and main actor was a remarkable achievement, and Vic thoroughly deserved all the accolades she received which included, of course, two BAFTAS, one for her writing and one for her acting.

One project that never came to fruition was the film *Calendar Girls* (2003, with Helen Mirren, Julie Walters and Celia Imrie). This is based on the real-life events in 1998 when a group of eleven middle-aged women aged forty-five to sixty-five from Rylstone and District WI in North Yorkshire who stripped off to produce a 'nude' calendar to raise money for a cancer charity.

It was tailor-made for Victoria. There were discussions with Vic, but in the end the film was made without her involvement either as writer or actor. What a pity! Apparently, some of the women involved thought it would turn out to be a 'star vehicle' for Vic. Surely it was obvious even then that Vic would never have done such a thing. She was always generous about giving her best lines to other actors, and she delighted in producing 'ensemble' pieces like *Acorn Antiques* and *dinnerladies*, in which she was just one of the cast. But for their own good reasons the Yorkshire lasses went with Disney.

But I must quote my favourite line from *Calendar Girls*:

we're going to need bigger buns!

That and

we're going to need a bigger boat

from the 1975 Steven Spielberg film *Jaws* have become part of the language. A gold star to the writers!

As she got older, Vic seemed more at ease with herself. In 2011 she told Chrissy Iley of *The Telegraph*:

I've had a very complicated life and now I don't worry about so many things. Moving into her sixties, Vic showed no signs of slowing down. She said: *It's more to do with the work than the exposure, the fame or the money. Work is crucial to my life. My creativity is what defines me. I feel I can work as hard as I ever did.*

On Boxing Day 2007 Vic appeared as 'Nana' in Granada's adaption of the Noel Streatfeild novel *Ballet Shoes*. Vic's last acting role was in voice only, as Inventrix in Sky1's animated cartoon version of *Fungus the Bogeyman* in December 2015, alongside Timothy Spall. In *Fungus*, a three part adaption of Raymond Briggs' 1977 children's picture book by scriptwriter Tom MacRae, Vic appears in voice only, which is maybe just as well. Fungus himself, voiced by Timothy Spall, is a disgusting, slimy green monster whose job it is to frighten human beings or 'dries'. Joanna Scanlan plays Fungus's wife Mildew, and Vic is the equally disgusting Inventrix. Bogeyman and his clan love dirt, grime and snot; they eat flies and maggots and fart a lot. Needless to say, this tale is loved by children of all ages.

So Vic did quite a lot of acting along the way. But there could have been more. Much, much more. Due to her final illness, Victoria was absent from the November screening of *Fungus*.

> **You know that building in London where all the windows blew out? That wasn't a bomb, it was fifty-six pre-menstrual women the day the chocolate machine broke down.**

If she had lived, Vic would surely have gone on to write and possibly produce and/or direct a major international film. One potential difficulty might have been her desire to keep everything under her own personal control. Any big film requires huge amounts of money, and the people who provide the money naturally want to have their say. This would not have suited Vic, who liked to be in control of every aspect of a production. This was not so much 'control-freakery' as a determination and a belief that you can't produce a good drama by committee.

Just as Vic disliked desk-bound TV executives trying to tell her what was and was not funny, Stan likewise was unhappy when his work was 'interfered with' as he saw it. In 1975 Stan wrote a terrific stage musical *Clogs!* based on Lancashire life, which was successfully produced at a number of northern theatres. It could and should have transferred to London's West End, but never did. I asked him why.

> *They want to own it* he said. *In this hard, commercial world, you can't expect anybody to put up a million pounds (or whatever) to put on a West End production, with no*

guarantee of a financial return and the possibility of a big loss, without having a big share of the 'vehicle'.

But Stan wouldn't 'let go' of his baby.

Vic had the fame, the money and the clout to get *Acorn Antiques* performed on the London stage, but even she would have had to give way to the moguls of Hollywood to get a major film on the screen.

I am sure that Vic, if she had lived, would have moved more into writing, producing and directing films: most likely British films, as I'm also sure Hollywood would not have been to her taste (despite Anne Reid's prediction of an Oscar!)

CHAPTER NINE

ERIC AND ERNIE

Vic and Geoff, who started life as a couple in a tiny flat in Morecambe, later moved to the tranquil village of Silverdale on the far side of Morecambe Bay. Silverdale is a lovely village at the end of a cul-de-sac, with a road leading down to the beach where there are great views over the Bay. It's a lovely house with its own orchard. The locals were hugely supportive of Vic and Geoff's wish to be allowed their privacy.

On my initial visit to see the Durham family at Silverdale with my wife Frances, we first called in at the local Post Office to enquire as to exactly where their cottage was: no satnavs in those days! The oldish couple behind the counter were very defensive. It was a bit like 'this is a local shop for local people' from *Little Britain*. 'Who are you and what do you want?' they demanded. Only when I could prove we were bona fide (or 'fide bono' as Vic would say on stage) did they release this precious information. No doubt hacks from London were given short shrift.

As idyllic as life in Silverdale was, Vic and Geoff found they were both having to spend a great deal of time in London, quite apart from being on the road performing and touring. With children Grace and Henry now at school, and their showbiz parents wanting to be with their kids as much as possible, Vic and Geoff made the decision - somewhat

" Do it again - properly this time "

reluctantly - to move to London. There they could be with the children much more, and there was also the children's education to think off.

My children won't eat chips. Some know-all at school told them a potato was a vegetable.

When the children were growing up, and particularly when they were very young, Vic did her best to tailor her work to enable her to be Mum to Grace and Henry as much as possible. When arranging a tour around various cities, she would book a hotel in a central location. After her show, Vic would return to the hotel each night so as to spend time with the kids next day. There were nannies of course, but Vic was always there for her children despite the huge demands on her time. Geoff too was a tower of strength and continued to be a close, caring father to his children even after he and Vic divorced in 2002, taking a house just round the corner.

> *I went to every concert, parents' evening, appointment and baby clinic. When I toured, which was only once every two years, the children sometimes came with me.*

Vic told *The Mail*

So the Wood-Durham family ended up in a beautiful Georgian House in upmarket Highgate in London. It fitted the bill exactly. Although close to the centre of the village, the house is discretely hidden behind a row of trees.

The only disadvantage I heard about living in Highgate came from the lips of Geoff, who has the most equitable temperament of anyone I know. Frances and I were visiting one Christmas when Geoff came in, all hot and bothered.

> *Do you know, I've been all up and down the High Street all morning and not one shop has any vegetarian suet!* he complained, *I suppose we'll just have to go to Harrods!*

> **I'm still emphatically single. You look at most middle-aged gentlemen and they tend to go out with ladies twenty years younger. If I was to find a gentleman it would probably be someone who's bombed Dresden.**

(Vic in 2015)

Eric and Ernie, with Victoria as Sadie Bartholomew, Eric

Morecambe's mother, was transmitted on BBC2 on New Year's Day 2011. Unusually, Victoria did not write the script, but she had great faith in the writer Peter Bowker and left it to him to write the screenplay after proposing the story. Daniel Rigby had the unenviable task of playing Eric Morecambe (Bartholomew) as a young man, with Brian Dick as the young Ernie Wise (Wiseman). Vic Reeves - another comic turned actor - played Eric's father George, and Reece Shearsmith Ernie's Dad Harry.

This marvellously-told tale was awarded the BAFTA for best single drama. Again, I was particularly pleased that Vic had shown herself more than capable of a dramatic acting role. More than once I urged Vic to do more serious acting, but - because of all the other things she wanted to do - it rarely happened.

My brother-in-law Geoffrey Durham also showed himself to be a more than capable actor in the 1987 British film *Wish You Were Here* with Emily Lloyd and Tom Bell, playing bus driver Harry Figgis with great aplomb. Again, I asked Geoff why he did not do more film work.

> *It's all right for the main actors,* he said, *but for the minor parts, it takes up a great deal of your time, there's a lot of waiting around, and you are not very well paid. It's just not worth it.*

From my very occasional appearances as a film extra, I can certainly attest to the low pay and the waiting around!

To me, Geoffrey Durham was tailor-made to be a hugely successful and popular TV game show host. It would have suited his personality perfectly. Geoff's TV persona was to be fat and jolly, but like Vic, he had his weight problems, and like Vic he overcame them. But a slimline Geoffrey looks a different person. Nevertheless, Geoffrey has had a very successful stage and TV career and continues to work 'in the business' as a much-sought after adviser and consultant.

Woman on a diet makes a panic call. Out shopping, she came face to face with a Marks & Spencer's individual spotted dick.

Vic wrote and directed *That Day We Sang* as a stage musical for the Manchester International Festival in 2011. It was revamped for television and shown on Boxing Day, 2014. Set in Manchester in 1929 and 1969, it's the engaging story of a middle-aged couple, Michael Ball (Tubby) and Imelda Staunton (Enid) who meet again after forty years at a reunion of the combined Manchester Schools Childrens Choir in which they sang *Nymphs and Shepherds* as ten-year olds. While that event had been hugely exciting, they had both led humdrum lives since. Needless to say, they rekindle the old excitement and - eventually - fall in love.

We went to see the stage production in Manchester, along with my cousin and her husband. As the writer and director, Vic was hugely engaged but still found time to pop in to see us in an adjoining coffee shop. Naturally, she could only stay a few minutes, something I fully appreciated, unlike my cousin who was a little put out. It's hard to explain to people the pressures that people like Vic are under. This was a new production, and as the writer and director, so much rested on Vic who would drive herself (and everybody else) relentlessly to ensure the best possible performance.

Vic was a guest on BBC TV *Breakfast* on November 25th 2014, along with actor Daniel Rigby who pays the stern-but-kind school teacher and choir master in the film version. Vic said her idea for *That Day We Sang* came from when, aged twenty-two and living in a Birmingham bedsit eating tins of mince, she saw a documentary about the reunion of a children's choir. It wasn't until 1988, some thirteen years later, that she started work on the project.

> *Something stayed with me from the documentary,* she said, *the idea of middle-aged people looking back at their lives, having had one very exciting day, reignites their love of music. As director, you are top of a pyramid of very clever people. You just rely on everybody else. It's my job to tell the story and keep my eye on what the script is about. I'm really trying to entertain people as best I can.*
>
> **All I do is put everything I can into the project and send it out to the world and wish that it is as entertaining as it can be.**

BBC2 on-line said:

> *Writer and director of* That Day We Sang, *Victoria Wood is highly regarded as one of Britain's best-loved comedians. She first came to prominence when she collaborated with Julie Walters in the sketches* Wood and Walters, Victoria Wood As Seen On TV, Pat and Margaret *and the award-winning* dinnerladies. *Victoria wrote and directed* That Day We Sang *for the 2011 Manchester International Festival. Here, she discusses her inspiration for the story and how she turned an acclaimed stage musical into a funny and heart-warming television drama.*

That Day We Sang *originally only had ten performances as a play, during the Manchester International Festival, and I always felt that it needed to have another life. So I went to the BBC and asked if it would be possible to turn it into a film and give it the opportunity to return. I knew about the children's choir recording* Nymphs and Shepherds *in the [Manchester] Free Trade Hall in 1929. Then when I was in my early twenties, I saw a documentary about the reunion of those choir members, forty-five years after they made that record. The idea popped into my head about people having a big, golden memory of something that had happened to them as a child and how perhaps their intervening lives did not yield that same level of joy.*

I liked the idea of the children's choir going to the Free Trade Hall to make a record, and how exciting that must have been for them. But the idea that really interested me was that of someone hearing themselves singing on the record forty-five years later, and being reconnected with the emotion that they had in their lives when they were ten. This is exactly what happens to our main character Tubby and sets up the driving force behind the story.

The heart of That Day We Sang *is music and the second chances of trying to find love. In 1929, Jimmy is auditioning for the Manchester school choir and makes a record. Running parallel to that story is the relationship between Tubby and Enid, who meet at a reunion of the choir. Tubby, in his overenthusiastic way, thinks he has a chance of a relationship with her and there are a few obstacles in the way of them getting together.*

All the musical numbers from the stage play are in the film, but two of them have been expanded upon and there is a new song for Enid. The orchestra was bigger in the stage version because we had the Hallé Youth Orchestra performing. For the film, we had a massive band organised by Tim Walker, but we did have the Hallé Youth Orchestra and the Hallé Children's Choir play Nymphs *and* Shepherds *as it was on the original record, so we got as near as we could to reproducing the original event.*

I thought Michael Ball would be perfect for the part.

I didn't want to direct the first few things that I had written as I didn't feel I had the capability. But over the years as I've done more things, more and more people have said I should direct and it started to feel like the right next step to take.

When we first started to cast for the original stage production, I thought Michael Ball would be perfect for the part.

We phoned his agent, who told us he was free which I found quite surprising! But it turns out we had phoned his acting agent; his singing agent told us he was booked up all year and unavailable. I am a massive fan of Imelda and have worked with her twice before, once in Kenya on Millennium Night *and she was in one of my Christmas specials the following year. She's an unusual combination of a powerful straight actress, but also very funny. I had seen her sing in* Cabaret *and she has a fantastic voice.*

Frank and Dorothy, the sidekicks to Tubby and Enid, were the next two important characters to cast. The characters are rather ghastly people who are hosting a viewing of the documentary at their posh modern house. Conleth Hill was perfectly cast as Frank. He is now known for doing Game Of

Thrones. *But I had seen him originally in* Stones In His Pockets *in the West End; an Irish play where Conleth played all the parts, including the women roles. It was a really brilliant performance, so I arranged for somebody to introduce me to him. Dorothy was harder to cast, but the moment Sophie Thompson came into read for it and sang the hell out of it, I knew it was her.*

All I do is put everything I can into the project and send it out to the world and wish that it is as entertaining as it can be. One of my favourite scenes is when Tubby and Enid are at the bus stop. It's nicely shot, the sky is quite grey and they are standing there in dull clothes. The music starts and Tubby sings Was that me? Did I sing? *I like the transition from talking to singing, especially when they are singing about not being able to sing; something you can only do in a musical. I wanted to create musical numbers in the film to echo the films that would have been in the world of Jimmy, Tubby and Enid.*

When Enid has a fantasy number, she is calling on those memories of seeing films like The Sheik *with Rudolph Valentino,* West Side Story *and* Sweet Charity *with Shirley MacLaine. We drew on America and Paris a lot for inspiration on the design of the dances, especially the use of painted backdrops for the fantasy numbers.*

I first met my choreographer, Sammy Murray Brown, when I had to learn how to tap dance for the Acorn Antiques *musical and I've worked with her ever since. She choreographed some beautiful numbers; the Ginger Rogers and Fred Astaire number where we have five couples dancing is stunning.*

The 60s period details are down to our brilliant designer Tom Burton. When we shot in Frank's house - a real house which we dressed with our own 60s props - all the cast and crew over a certain age went around saying: 'ooh we had one of those!' To have an idea and see that come to life in any form is very lucky. So I was extremely lucky to be given the opportunity to make That Day We Sang *into a stage piece and a film.*

I think The Sound of Music *is a brilliant film though I don't actually like it. I love the score of* Gypsy *- I recently saw a brilliant performance by Imelda as Rose -* Guys and Dolls, Hairspray *and* The Book of Mormon. *I'm rather fond of* Bedknobs and Broomsticks *just because I used to watch it a lot with my children.*

I couldn't tell you what audiences take away from anything that I do. I hate having to say what's good about something I've written - but I can quite happily advise people to watch That Day We Sang *because the central performances of Michael and Imelda are so beautiful and moving - and we have a great cast in Sophie Thompson, Vincent Franklyn, Conleth Hill, Dorothy Atkinson, Jessica Gunning and Daniel Rigby.*

Not all the critics were kind. Tim Martin of *The Telegraph* wrote:

What we got instead was a sweet but saggy drama, held together by spot-on performances from Michael Ball, Imelda Staunton and their colleagues, but with a plot and tunes sloshing about in more schmaltz than you'd find at a chicken-soup convention.

In 2012 *The Telegraph*'s Ben Lawrence interviewed Victoria when she was filming the BBC drama *Loving Miss Hatto* - a true-life story about a terminally ill pianist whose doting husband passed off recordings by famous concert pianists as hers in order to give her some solace. He wrote:

> *a typical Wood story about small-town dreams. It was strange to be in the presence of someone I had watched regularly since childhood - blonde bob, piercing blue eyes, soft, slightly scornful voice. She was not quite what I expected; I found her rather reserved. But then we took a break and started looking at the photographs that hung on the wall of Dublin's Olympia Theatre where she was filming.*

Once again, Victoria found herself under pressure writing *Mrs Hatto*. She told *The Telegraph*'s Chrissy Iley:

> *I did enjoy writing it* [That Day We Sang] *but I felt under a lot of time pressure. I finished it only last Wednesday because I was writing something else at the same time.*

That 'something else' was Vic's 2012 screenplay about pianist Joyce Hatto who caused a storm of controversy after her death when it was revealed that many of her recordings were not entirely by her. 'I've just torn myself away from the desk to come here,' explains Wood, her forehead furrowed with tension. 'It's awful doing two things at once. Horrible. I keep forgetting that

> *I don't do much acting. I didn't write* Eric & Ernie.

But it was her idea and she was a producer, and many assumed she did write it because she gave such an incredible performance as the stage mother who held Morecambe and Wise together. Paul Allen wrote in the *Guardian*:

It incorporated a wealth of human disillusion and more comic one-liners than is altogether fair in a sad, sad story.' Its problem, he wrote, was that it was sometimes *'too knicker-wettingly funny.*

Reflecting on *Mrs Hatto*, Vic said:

I had to take a line with something that has been proved to be illegal. Left Bank Pictures asked me to write it, about a fraud. Vic decided not to meet the husband, but to keep herself at a distance. *I had to keep a barrier in my head, I wanted to keep a clean sheet.* Instead, Vic talked to people who had met the husband. *There was a huge amount of research. It took for ever, since 2009.*

Victoria pours Morrisey 'a nice cup of tea'

48 Music Hall star Marie Lloyd was originally named Victoria Wood

49 Early comedy style

50 New Faces 1974

51 That's Life 1976

52 Summer Show 1975

53 Wood & Walters 1983 (GettyImages)

54 Jules and Vick enjoy a cup of tea

*55 Cast of dinnerladies 1998
(l-r) at back: Duncan Preston,
Andrew Dunn; front: Anne Reid,
Thelma Barlow, Victoria Wood, Julie
Walters, Celia Imrie, Shobna Gulati*

*56 With Julie as Mrs Overall
(Acorn Antiques 1985)*

57 Julie and Victoria as Pat and Margaret 1994

58 With Thora Hird

59 Premiere of TV film That Day We Sang *2014: (l-r) Paul Frift (producer), Michael Ball (actor), Victoria Wood (writer and director), Hilary Bevan Jones (executive producer)*

60 With Duncan Preston

61 With Daniel Rigby (Eric and Ernie 2010)

62 Women in Film and Television Awards 2008: so pleased when close friend and colleague Julie Walters received the EON Lifetime Achievement Award (Victoria got the same award in 2011)

63 Judith Chalmers (r) gets up close and personal with Victoria and Gloria Hunniford

64 With writer Alan Bennett (l) and actor Richard Griffiths (GettyImages)

65 With Dame Judi Dench and Dench's daughter, actress Finty Williams

66 Red Nose Day with Spice Girl Geri Halliwell

67 At the Women of the Year Awards

68 With husband Geoffrey Durham

69 Grace and Henry Durham
with Mum Victoria

70 Celebrating her CBE
with children Henry and Grace 2008

71 No-nonsense hairstyle

72 With Yehudi Menuhin, 125th birthday of the Royal Albert Hall

*73 At David Frost's annual
summer garden party*

74 London Fashion Week

75 Victoria liked her scarves

76 Double BAFTA success, Housewife, 49 2007

*77 Handbag needed for
BAFTA awards night*

78 Happy to win

*79 British Comedy
Awards 2000*

81 Jolly and relaxed

80 The Secret Policeman's Other Ball *for Amnesty International 1981 (GettyImages)*

82 Proud to be awarded the CBE 2008

83 Confident and secure (GettyImages)

Except where indicated, all photographs in this section are the property of Photoshot

CHAPTER TEN

AN AUDIENCE WITH...

Perhaps the greatest accolade any performer can be given is to star in their own *An Audience With...* TV show. Victoria's turn came on 10th December 1988, the London Weekend Television (LWT) programme produced and directed by David Hillier. The programme won Vic another BAFTA, and it was voted the favourite female comedy performance in a *TV Times* poll.

Before an audience of her peers, with dozens and dozens of famous faces from TV, stage and film, Victoria gave a tour de force of the very best from her stand-up and TV shows. It was just her and a piano, and an audience laughing fit to bust. With her machine-gun delivery, the audience scarcely had time to laugh before Victoria was on to her next funny line. As usual, it was a mixture of old and new.

Seventy-two baps - Connie you slice, I'll spread.

'Mensa was shut, was it?' (to 'thinking man's crumpet', TV presenter Joan Bakewell); 'I've come on the Manchester Shuttle, it's very old, I had to sit next to the rear gunner'; 'When I was at the Edinburgh Festival, I had to share a dressing-room with Rudolph Nureyev. I used to kip in his hammock - at least I think it was his hammock'; 'Christmas shopping - men are hopeless. They go into the lingerie department to get a pair of French knickers for their wives, but they try and do it without looking or touching them, or

165

saying the name'; (as 'Sandra'): 'I couldn't get you a strawberry yoghurt, so I got you a meat and potato pie'; And when someone dies, we say 'seventy-two baps - Connie you slice, I'll spread'.

Victoria used a format that has become standard for many comics, and which she had honed to perfection: the running story, interrupted by gags and non-sequiturs before returning to her original tale, sometimes having to remind her audience that she is returning to the main story. This was a (very) tall tale about a man chasing her from a supermarket.

She quips that some people mistake her for Dawn French 'what's it like being married to Lenny Henry?' or for a character from *Fresh Fields*, a TV sitcom starring Julia McKenzie and Anton Rogers. 'Julia McKenzie?' she asks, 'no, the small fat one in the corner' is the reply.

Eye shadow comes this season in all shades of the speculum.

'The Introvert's Burger - just a serviette but they don't like to say anything'; 'I lived with a married man once, as man and wife. It was just like a proper marriage: no sex and lots of arguments'; (as a department store beauty therapist): 'eye shadow comes this season in all shades of the speculum'.

Vic played and sang one of her many songs about disappointed love,

Things would never have worked - Your idea of foreplay was to take your socks off.

To great applause, Vic appears among the audience as 'Kimberley's friend' in orange mac and yellow beret.

I'm looking for my fwend, Kimberley. 'Ave you seen 'er? She's very, very tall, and very, very broad';

Mrs Gupta's a really nice woman. She comes from somewhere far away that has a funny name - Kidderminster;

As a researcher with clipboard, doing a survey in the street (as her mother Nellie used to do for real) 'totally bona fide'.

Of course Victoria just had to finish with *The Ballad of Barry and Freda* (aka *Let's Do It!*) and the audience were not disappointed. They went wild!

He's not really my husband, but he did rub up against me in a sports coat so he's as good as.

When Victoria died, there was much discussion about why she had not been made a dame. Esther Rantzen, herself a dame, was adamant. She told the *Mail* that Victoria should have been a dame, says Esther:

Broadcaster questions why comic never received the honour. Dame Esther gave Wood an early break on her show *That's Life!* Victoria was twice recognised by the Queen for her contributions to the world of entertainment but was never given a damehood. Hours after Wood lost her secret six-month battle with cancer on Wednesday, the seventy-five year-old broadcaster told BBC Breakfast:

The thing about her humour was that even though it was very sharp, very clear-eyed, it was never cruel. She was never obscene, even though she was mischievous.

Dame Esther received her title in 2015 for services to young people as the founder of charities ChildLine and The Silver Line.

The *Mail's* Richard Barber recalled a 2014 interview with Victoria:

So, Dame Julie [Walters] one day, I ventured? 'Oh, she's got to be. In fact, why's she not one already?' Which also begged the question: wasn't it about time she was Dame Victoria?

> I don't want to be,' she said, *but it would depend on what my children wanted. If the kids said, 'Oh Mum, that's so embarrassing,' then I'd turn it down. On the other hand, if they really wanted me to have it, then I'd say yes.*

I suggested on one occasion that the words 'national' and 'treasure' were increasingly attached to her name.

> And I disown them,' she shot back. *Everyone's a national treasure these days; you can't move for them. But there should only be one at a time. For years, it was Thora Hird. After she died it was going to be Judi Dench but Joanna Lumley saved the Gurkhas so she got the gig.*
>
> **No one's ever seen me with a footballer or falling out of a limo with no pants on.**

Barber wrote that Victoria was the least starry A-lister you could hope to meet.

> I'm very low-rent,' she confided. 'I like going to Foyles and buying a new book in hardback. I go first class on the train but only on a plane if it's long-haul. In London I travel by tube or bus and nobody faints with horror. Anyway, what are they going to do? Smile at you? But then there's nothing interesting about me. No one's ever seen me with a footballer or falling out of a limo with no pants on. And those below a certain age don't know who I am.*

Guardian reader Michael Byrne from Reading said in a letter to the paper:

> *Surely I cannot be the only one to demand that Victoria Wood be given a state funeral. Maggie Thatcher was granted one for destroying our society. Victoria added to our sense of wellbeing and humanity.*

> **People think I hate sex. I don't. I just don't like things that stop you seeing the television properly.**

In the BAFTA award ceremony shortly after Victoria's death, she was the first person mentioned in 'those who have left us' spot. Award winner Michaela Coel paid tribute to Victoria during her acceptance speech. Michaela won her second BAFTA for the best female performance in a comedy prize for her role in E4's *Chewing Gum*. As she took to the stage, she started her speech by saying:

> *I would like to pay my respects to Victoria Wood, with [this award] in my hand.*

Later ITV re-broadcast *Let's Do It!: A Tribute To Victoria Wood*, first shown immediately after her death, 'a tour de force of comic songs and sharp wit'. John Robinson of the *Guardian* wrote:

> *The gathering here is a sadder occasion, to celebrate her life after her passing several weeks ago. Clips abound, while tributes come from co-stars and famous faces such as Peter Kay, Celia Imrie and David Threlfall.*

In April 2002 *The Independent's* Rachel Halliburton wrote:

> *Having a hysterectomy proved an unexpected gift to Victoria Wood. The ordeal of hormonal ups and downs, intrusive gynaecological examinations, and sterilised*

surgical probings all proved a rich source of inspiration for her latest and final stand-up show, At It Again. *In her routine she describes a consultant who walked into her hospital room with a crowd of students, and plunged his arm inside her with the directness a vet normally reserves for a cow. 'I said, 'Look, I don't expect you to take me out to dinner first, but hello would be nice'.' It is, Wood reveals with some pride, 'a filthy show, very surgical. It proves there's nothing you can't say if you say it in the right way'.*

A hysterectomy does seem the perfect subject matter for a comedian who has etched her reputation around the insecurities, anxieties and ridiculous pressures faced by women, whether she is describing the librarian reduced to blind-dating a mechanical engineer with a charisma bypass and Hush Puppies, or the girl caught short on a country ramble without enough chocolate to power her across the landscape. She would not, you feel, describe herself as a feminist - Wood would be less interested in burning a bra than making fun of the thermal underwear section in the catalogue it came from. She maintains a quiet northern determination to avoid ponceyness in any form - a woman who might well call a tea cosy a tea cosy, her piercingly observed comic domain is stubbornly suburban.

Foreplay is like beefburgers - three minutes on each side.

Her world has filtered into the nation's consciousness, whether it is satirising aspects of the women's self-help industry, discussing sex, Woman's Weekly *style, sending up soap-opera or relishing the comic potential of words and phrases such as candlewick, carpet-rod, fruit-and-nut, or gingham wrap-around.*

Jude Kelly wrote that Victoria:

Observed the banality of ordinary life so well because she had lived that life, and felt real affection for it. Before women like Catlin Moran or Jo Brand came along, talking about periods or chocolate, she was already covering that territory, discussing whether you buy one or two pairs of knickers for a trip to Blackpool, and do you wash one pair and hang them out at night. She understood the minutiae of women's concerns and nailed those insecurities, in a tradition of singular women including Joyce Grenfell, Marie Lloyd, Beryl Reed, and Lucille Ball.

In her 2013 BBC two-part special *Victoria Wood's Nice Cup of Tea*, Vic reveals how tea is made East and West. In Episode 2 (April 3rd 2013) Victoria shares a cuppa with Graham Norton, Matt Smith and Morrisey. TV host Norton and Vic, sitting in comfortable armchairs, drank tea in front of the telly.

It's not just a drink says Vic: We're not good at talking, so tea is a substitute.

Vic has tea with *Dr Who* star Matt Smith in Claridges

I love the ritual.

In the 1950s came commercial television and the ad break, two minutes to make a cup of tea.

Serena Davies of *The Telegraph* commented:

The funniest line was when, after a Chinese waitress had recited a little speech lasting around thirty seconds as she presented Wood with her lunch, Wood summarised it as 'Minestrone's off'. But actually, even if the programme wasn't pitched at the most sophisticated level, Wood's presence, frequently self-deprecating, always warm, was a pleasure throughout.

Therapy is like getting your car mended.

Victoria has twice been the castaway on *Desert Island Discs*. The first was with Michael Parkinson on 3rd February 1987. Parkinson introduced Vic as

a very funny woman, the Nissan of joke writing, actor, comedian, playwright, scriptwriter, musician, composer.

In her chat, Vic said:

I like to be on my own better than with other people. I can swim quite a long way, but I probably wouldn't (try to escape) I'd be too frightened. Mostly mood music to put me in a good mood remind me of other things. Music played a huge part. I was never good at anything else. I joined a brass band at twelve or thirteen. That was a great time. I played second trumpet. I could either play or march, but not both, so I had to drop out.

Father was an insurance underwriter, a very northern occupation, no clogs. We were an ordinary middle-class family. It was very boring, all I did was play the piano, eating and watching the box. At first I wanted to be a boxer and then I wanted to be famous. At fifteen I joined Rochdale Youth Theatre. I started to get parts in plays, always funny parts. I thought 'I can do this'. I was really lazy at home. (third movement of Prokofiev's Seventh Symphony*) a great tune, used to play it all the time.*

We rented a flat. I found my husband dyeing his stage shoes. He spilt shoe polish on the pale green carpet. After that we nearly got divorced. I was on the dole for so long, I wanted to earn a living. You have to have a certain amount of fame to do your job. People poke you, it's part of the job. There're always mixing you up with other people.

At seventeen and a half in my only school play I played Autolycus in A Winter's Tale. *I had these horrible brown tights. I had only two GCE 'O' Levels. Birmingham was the only place barmy enough to take me in. There was lots of acting all done by tall blonde girls. I was told to be stage manager. (Fats Waller's African Ripples) I can't play with both hands. Tutors told me not to do it. I auditioned for the only female part in* Loot. *I didn't get it, so I was told to play the piano at the end as the audience. As they were walking out, I said 'don't go'. I played this song I had written about how I should have got the part.*

At seventeen I auditioned for Manchester Poly School of Theatre. I was ill with nerves the whole time. Julie (Walters) gave an impression of a nurse with a commode. I thought she was really funny. In 1978 met (again). I did a double take. She said:

'You were the girl who kept throwing up'.

My audition piece was the Juliet death scene. It was so stupid, me with glasses, Lancashire accent and a mini skirt. I did improve and did a bit of movement.

I worry about having a baby in case it grows up and can't find a parking space.

Ian Dury and Noël Coward are the only people with lyrics I listen to. My boyfriend had ditched me when I went in for Pub Entertainer of the Year, which was funny as I didn't go into pubs and I wasn't funny. I came third out of five first came three enormous girls in enormous hot pants, second a man dressed as a skeleton who came out of a cardboard coffin and sang Take off your skin and dance in your bones. I wanted to show him I could get on without him.

In New Faces I did win one heat. We were all given the most appalling Summer Show, a really bad variety show. We got £125 a week. Marti Caine complained - I thought it was marvellous. After that I was in the doldrums. I would write songs for Pebble Mill. The man at the BBC told me a song had to be two minutes ten seconds, so for years every song I wrote was 2 minutes 10 seconds, silly.

I've given up trying to feed my children. I just point at the grill and fish-fingers and tell them to get on with it.

What got me going was Roger McGough and John Dowie and I started working in the theatre. Death at the Bush was the first thing I was asked to do, four songs, write three songs and a sketch. It was the only funny sketch, it was a very serious show and it got all the reviews. It was the first thing I had properly done and it gave me a big lift.

It's very difficult to do both playwright and have an act. Noël Coward Live in Las Vegas with Let's Do It! With a most unlikely audience he works them up and makes a killing. My TV career, a play at Sheffield Crucible. Producer Peter Eckersley was just about to do the series when he died. He was the perfect person to meet at that stage. I knew Eckersley for four years. I was knocked back when he died.

I'm always writing things down as I hear them but never use them. It's invented. It's nice to be when everyone else isn't. I do like to keep away from other comics. I can get a lot more work done and there's more social life down there (London), *here people know I can work all day and in the evening if necessary.*

My BBC TV series has just ended. Six shows takes six months, with twice as much as we need, enough to throw away. Audiences in London are the coldest, when I first started I had some appalling audiences, falling asleep. Smallest: seven peopled outside Birmingham, one was a man on a portable life support machine. Live performance is the hardest and most enjoyable. You really have to do your best. People have paid to see you. It's their night out.

The Royal Variety Show *was a big laugh, a little bit crowded backstage. I would like to go to the USA and Australia where they will show my first two series together next year. The Weather Girls - two enormous black girls with two enormous black voices. I am a mad walker with my Walkman.* Fats Waller, *I can try and learn with both hands.*

For my book, the collected works of Arthur Marshall. *He's the only one who makes me laugh when I'm on my own. My luxury, a cinema organ, a mighty Wurlitzer I can learn and have a good time.*

Vic's choice of music:

Disc 1. Jack Brymer playing Eric Coates' *Saxo-Rhapsody in A minor*.

Disc 2. *Prokofiev* part of the third movement of the Seventh Symphony with the Esland Symphony orchestra conducted by Andre Previn

Disc 3. Fats Waller *African Ripples* (last disc to keep)

Disc 4. Ian Dury and the Blockheads *Inbetweenies*

Disc 5. George Gershwin part of the first movement of his *Concerto in F* played by Andre Previn with the London Symphony Orchestra

Disc 6. Noël Coward *Live in Las Vegas Let's Do It!*

Disc 7. Buddy Berigan playing Bix Beiderbeck's *In a Mist*

Disc 8. The Weather Girls *Lock Me Up*

It was not Hitler's intention in invading Poland (just) to liberate Nella Last.

The second was on Dec 22nd 2007 with Kirsty Young who introduced Vic as:

Writer, actress, composer, stand-up comedienne. After twenty-five years of sell-out tours, stage shows and a successful sitcom, she has written and starred in a drama, Housewife, 49. She once said that comedy is about making people like you: she is adored.

Vic said she was comfortable with her fame:

You go into TV or show business for the attention. I was very happy that night (she got the two BAFTAS for Housewife, *49). It's a nod that you have achieved something. Next day I thought about something else. The two BAFTAS were quite heavy.*

Granada asked me to produce something, and I thought it would make a good drama. The war liberated her: it was not Hitler's intention in invading Poland (just) to liberate Nella Last.

Randy Newman is my hero. Marie is a very, very simple song. He writes such beautiful music, I stopped writing songs for a bit. I started again when I decided to write a

musical.

I'm always crying. We were an unusual family, my upbringing in a massive bungalow on top of a hill. It had been an anti-aircraft base. I had my own room with a piano, a TV and my books. I made my own food. After a point we never really sat round the table. Food wasn't made. I had a huge eating problem. Our home absolutely crammed with books. We never, ever had any visitors. I was an obsessive reader and a more than obsessive eater. I wasn't miserable, but I was quite isolated. It didn't help learning to be with people. Mother was very depressed. Father was away working: when he was home he was writing. We never talked about anything. It was windswept, bleak. Mother was depressed. She was always on a diet or overeating.

Joyce Grenfell made a huge impression on me. I was six or seven, seeing a woman standing alone on the stage. Mother said you can't go, you're too small. Grenfell came out to see me, I have never forgotten. When I do a show, I always go to the stage door. Birdland by Weather Report, you can sing along with it, it's very jolly. The live version, my son decided on it.

I was very clever, a smart little girl, top of the class in primary school. I couldn't deal with everyone else being just as clever.

Some mornings I sit up in bed convinced my brain has fallen out in the night and I've lost it somewhere under the pillow.

I couldn't do homework, it was just a big mess. I was not the class clown, I didn't have any friends, a bit of a misfit. I did a lot of observing, I was still reading all the time and at the piano. When I was about seven, father wrote the names of the notes in pencil on the keys to Polly Wolly Doodle, *and on the music and I worked it out by decode. After that I was obsessed with the piano. I feel really sorry for her (me as a little girl). She was neglected.*

Thank the Lord for Rochdale Council Youth Theatre Workshop. *My sister (Rosalind) was at school in Rochdale. When I was fifteen it was like the sun came out. I thought, I'm in the right place where your personality is of value. It was just fantastic, I felt comfortable on stage. Inside was a very, very furious streak of ambition. I had a very serious belief in myself that I could be very good at being funny. When I sat (at the piano) on my own with no-one around I would twist round as if for an audience.*

Violinist Gidon Kremer playing Solidad *lowers my heart rate, I relax. I decided I wanted to go to Drama School. I had an audition at Manchester Poly. I was sick as a dog all day, saw an odd-looking very small girl with lots of brown hair with a clip-board (Julie Walters). She was really fun. I did get to know her, we met at Shepherd's Bush seven years later. We got on really well. I had always thought about her.*

Slim blonde girls from the Home Counties who knew about Shostakovich. *University drama not a sausage. Worst degree you can get. Chunky boots big coats loads of hair. When twenty auditions and* New Faces, *I had quite a lot of initiative, an audition* Pebble Mill. *My act was a few songs, little topical songs, sitting down. It took me a few years to progress to stand up.* Mr Scruff Get A Move On: *my son is up to the minute on pop music my favourite track.*

We had twenty-six years together. We met at the Phoenix Theatre, Leicester. He was an actor, Buffalo Bill. I was musical director show he was in. It was just one of those things. We just clicked in every way. He was encouraging. My comedy was different. To be without somebody in your corner is really lonely. We did everything together.

There's no formula to writing. It took me from 1974 to 1978 to work out how to write a joke. I knew when I did it I though, aha!

To be able to make people laugh is the nicest thing you can do for somebody really - apart from a blow-job or something.

At the Bush Theatre I just suddenly saw the way to construct a sentence so the people had to get a laugh. I did want to be on stage, it's more interesting. I don't just want to write and hand it over. In 1978 did a sketch with Julie in another theatre. She auditioned for the main part and got it. Tom Waits with Misery is the River of the World *makes me laugh even though it's gloomy. It's based on truth. Stand-up is in reality you try and be honest but in the end it's two hours of lies.*

The Doobie Brothers What a Fool Believes. *This is my happy music warm-up track. I absolutely love it. I'm quite happy to talk about it (my weight. I am very, very anti the dieting industry. They exploit people's insecurities, they don't deliver what they promise.*

I was on a diet pills fully at twelve and thirteen. I used to buy those terrible things that look like custard creams. Mother was on them as well. I was always obsessing,

obsessing about my weight. It doesn't ever go away. Not till I was around forty. I was using food as a drug, as a distraction, avoidance. I just felt ashamed about being fat. I deal with it better than I used to.

Tabula Rasa *by the Kris Chamber Orchestra. This is one of my favourites. When I had a very bad time it would take away the numb feeing. I used to play it when it was a bad time. I felt like a cartoon character who steps off a cliff and their legs are still going but there's nothing underneath. Twenty-six years is a long time. I found it (divorce) very difficult. The landscape changes. I found it comforting to talk to a therapist. Food is very comforting.*

I wrote music, joyful jokes, the Acorn Antiques *musical which is odd. The first thing I did was to write some jolly tunes. I could never talk about my marriage on stage. Here's some dear old Dame Julie Walters - could do (doing) eight shows, Monday night and Wednesday matinees, a hell of a job eight shows a week.*

My daughter goes to Clare College [Cambridge] next year. If she gets on the CD that will make my Christmas. (My choice of book) has to be Dickens, he wrote nice big books. I'll be too fine. (I'll have) a bumper book of Sudoku with every other page blank, with a nice black pen I don't do workings-out. The Dooby Brothers make me smile.

Vic's choice of music:

Disc 1. Randy Newman *Marie*

Disc 2. Weather Report *Birdland*

Disc 3. Violinist Gidon Kremer *Solidad* (only Vic chose this)

Disc 4. Mr Scruff *Get A Move On*

Disc 5. Tom Waits *Misery is the River of the World*

Disc 6. Doobie Brothers *What a Fool Believes* (one track to keep)

Disc 7. Arvo Pärt *Tabula Rasa* Kris Chamber Orchestra

Disc 8. Clare College Singers Carol orchestrated and conducted by John Rutter

Victoria's top five tracks, as played on the BBC:

1. *Barry & Freda*

2. *What We Find*

3. *The Ballad of Barry & Freda* (*Let's Do It!*)

4. *The Smile Song*

5. *dinnerladies* theme

Professional northerners live in Barnes.

In 1990 Vic went to Ethiopia to make a documentary about how Comic Relief money had been spent. She returned in 1995 and lived with a Masari family in Chivi, Zimbawbwe, milking cows, weeding vegetable plots, making clay drainpipes and digging troughs. In 1991 Vic made a Comic Relief comedy record with comedy duo Hale & Pace with *Stonk*. Vic's *the Smile Song* was on the flip side. It reached No. 1 in the UK charts in March 1991. In February 1990 Vic made the *Money Well Spent* Comic Relief documentary in Ethiopia. Vic did more for Comic Relief in 1999, and in 2003 she took part in the Playtex Moonwalk.

Vic's 1992 Christmas Day show was called *Victoria Wood's All-*

Day Breakfast. In September 1996 she was featured on the LWT *South Bank Show*. In 2011 Vic made one the documentary series of *Great Railway Journeys* for the BBC, but instead of a glamorous foreign location she chose *Crewe to Crewe*. She won the *Comic Relief Bake Off* in 2015. Vic did a good deal of TV advertising. In 1982 she filmed an advert in the Bahamas for diet drink One-Cal. She has also done ads for McVities chocolate digestives and Dyson cleaners.

In April 1993 Vic ended a seven-month tour ending with fifteen nights at the Albert Hall. In 2001 it was a sixty-five date tour, and the following year saw Vic *At It Again* with twenty-three dates. She could fill halls anywhere in the UK, and regularly did so. Vic still did the occasional acting job, playing the tea lady in Terry Jones' 1996 film of *Wind in the Willows* with Jones, Steve Coogan and Eric Idle. In 2011 Vic played Granny Driver in the TV movie *The Borrowers* with Christopher Eccleston.

In April 1996 Vic told *OK* Magazine:

> *I think a lot of shy people are really egomaniacs who haven't actually found a way to communicate with people,, so they choose circumstances where they are in control and can set the agenda. Performing is the perfect job for a shy person. They can say exactly what they want to say whereas in a social situation they might be clumsy or tongue-tied. I am not very adept at parties, but put me on the stage at the Albert Hall and I can cope.*

Vic also said:

> *I'm very unadventurous. When I play 'Monopoly' I always buy the stations and utilities. It was only about last year*

when I found out how to pronounce 'Marylebone'. I still don't like saying it to taxi drivers. I'd rather be dropped off on the Euston Road and walk. **(Lucky Bag)**

Counselling was like polishing your shoes, only it costs more or like tidying your knicker drawer.

After Vic died, Chris Hastings, Art Correspondent for the *Mail on Sunday*, wrote that

Vic had been denied an honour four times. She got the OBE in 1997 after Labour came to power and the CBE in 2008. Government ministers give their order of preference in various fields: in 1994 she was ranked sixth in the entertainment field, but in the two lists of 1996 she had fallen to 12th and 7th. Hastings points out that she poked fun at then Prime Minister John Major, his wife Norma, and his government in her sell-out shows. In one routine she described the then Foreign Secretary Douglas Hurd as looking 'like someone very high up in the carpet department at Selfridges', and in another she joked that the 1991 mortar attack on Downing Street was an attempt by Margaret Thatcher to recover the curtains from Major. During a tour in 1993 she described Norma Major as the 'sort of woman who has a separate J-cloth for each bath tap'.

Did these quips have an effect? We can only speculate.

In 2013 the TV panel quiz show *QI*, hosted by know-all Stephen Fry, announced:

Victoria Wood is comic royalty and it's no surprise to discover she once beat the Queen Mum into second place in a 'person you'd most like to live next door to you' poll.

We've long coveted her as a QI panellist: her combination of personal warmth and brilliant comic timing is just so right for the format. But Victoria is a famously shy and private person and doesn't really do panel shows. Also, as one of the nation's favourite dramatists, musicians, actresses and comedians, she's usually busy producing wonderful original work of her own. But, after a decade of gentle coaxing, Victoria finally appeared amidst the spoons and forks and turnspit dogs of the Kitchen show. Whether playing comic or serious roles, the core to Victoria Wood's appeal is her ability to instantly make you feel that she's an old friend. 'I think a lot of very seemingly shy people have got this ability to connect with a group, rather than one-on-one', she recently told the Guardian. *'And I just knew, I just knew I had that I couldn't define it, but I knew I had it'*

(QI) Episode 13 December 15th 2013

The audience is the only thing.

Asked about how she judges her material, Vic said:

'The audience is the only thing'. She would try it out with a small audience, 'a tiny bit of new stuff with a whole load of old stuff, and just hope for the best. We are so bad at enjoying ourselves.

In the *Radio Times* of June 1980, Judi Goodwin described Victoria as

the working girls' Joyce Grenfell.

The *Mail*'s Jack Tinkler said:

try to imagine a combination of Joyce Grenfell and Gracie Fields delivering a one-woman tribute to the art of Joan Rivers.

All I'm concerned about is that audiences enjoy my shows.

Vic told the November 1986 _Radio Times_:

> I don't think I could write something and just hand it over to someone else to do because that's the fun bit, putting a bit of lippy on and getting out there! I was very pleased to win (the BAFTA) but it really put pressure on me. I was already writing the new series and every time I looked at the award I kept thinking that people would be expecting so much more now and I just wouldn't be able to live up to it. In the end, I just had to put the thing away.

She told the Manchester Evening News:

> All I'm concerned about is that audiences enjoy my shows.

Vic told the _Mirror_:

> I just shut myself away at home with my piano and get on with it. I work office hours, nine to five-ish, and make myself do it. It really is fun doing the shows. I enjoy the performing bit - but the writing is hell. I was very undisciplined in my university days and did as little work as possible. Two years after New Faces I was still broke and living in a bedsit. I thought 'I'm twenty-three and I've blown it'.

Vic was on the front cover of _TV Quick_ in November 1991:

> Half my act used to be about Morecambe, but you can't live in a place just to get material. Alan Bennett lives in bloody Camden Town, for God's sake, and he's been writing plays about Yorkshire for the last twenty-nine years.

In 1993 she was on the front cover of _You_ magazine

> Tricky Vicky, an audience with the Queen of Comedy wrote

Angela Levin. When I asked about her parents' reaction to her success, caused her features to tighten and her face to become almost immobile.

(*The Mail on Sunday*) June 27th

Miss Wood can put more funny lines into a ten-minute scene than most writers manage in an hour.

The Listener, 1980

The only reason I'd like people to recognise me is that it would show I was a success. Being successful means you're good at your job, and more than anything else I want that, said Vic.

" Music and Laughter in Heaven "

CHAPTER ELEVEN

FAREWELL TO A GENIUS

When my sister Victoria Wood died on April 20th 2016, there was a massive outpouring of grief and love. Not since the death of 'Princess Di' - Lady Diana Spencer - nearly twenty years earlier had there been such a display of emotion from all walks of society. Again, a tsunami of grief and love swept the country.

'National Treasure' intoned Prime Minister David Cameron, among many others. 'Funniest ever woman'; 'the person you'd most like to live next door to'; 'one of the greats'; 'the very definition of funny bones'; 'The most loyal and lovely friend you could ever wish for'; 'unparalleled comedy genius'; 'There will never be another'; 'A true comedy icon'.

Like Diana, the 'People's Princess', Victoria was greatly loved, but she was also hugely admired for entertaining us right royally with both comedy and drama in a career spanning forty years that encompassed stand-up comedy, TV shows, films and musicals. Vic excelled as a singer-songwriter, comedian, actor, producer and director. She blazed a trail for female comics, the first woman to make it as a stand-up, the first comic of either sex to sell out the Royal Albert Hall with a solo show for fifteen consecutive nights.

What made Victoria's successful career in so many different fields all the more remarkable was that she wrote all her own material, scripts, stories, jokes, music.

Victoria's success did not come easily. Not only did she have years of struggle, she had to endure a lonely and unhappy childhood living in an isolated house, largely ignored by her parents. There were no family meals: Vic ate in her own room. Our mother Nellie suffered from depression and never encouraged her daughter, and when our Dad Stan, insurance man, part-time scriptwriter and playwright, wasn't away working, he was busy writing in his study. Both mother and daughter took diet pills, constantly battling against being overweight.

From an early age, Vic harboured a burning ambition to entertain, but she had no idea how to do it. So, how did this lonely, unhappy, overweight girl become one of the best loved and most popular entertainers of our era? In the end, it was down to Vic herself. Certainly, she had a huge amount of inborn talent, but it is entirely due to Vic's own character and single-minded determination to succeed from very unpromising beginnings that she reached the pinnacle of success and stayed there for decades.

Vic's road to success in so many different fields is a fascinating story. It's my privilege to be able to tell that story from the unique perspective of being her elder brother. While I hugely admire everything that Vic has achieved and count myself one of her greatest fans, she did have her faults - as do we all. As an author and biographer I have always tried to tell the whole story of the people I have written about, 'warts and all', and with Vic it is no different.

When the BBC announced that Victoria Wood had died, it was almost as if she had been a member of the royal family:

Comedian Victoria Wood has died aged sixty-two after a short battle with cancer. Victoria passed away on April 20th after a short battle with cancer.

Her publicist, Neil Reading, said:

Victoria Wood has sadly passed away, after a short but brave battle with cancer. The multi BAFTA award-winning writer, director, actor and comedian died peacefully at her north London home with family this morning.

The Beeb went on to say:

Victoria Wood inspired a new generation of female comics in a hugely successful career on television and on stage.

After Victoria's death, her team posted one of her best lines on Twitter:

Life's not fair is it? Some of us drink champagne in the fast lane and some of us eat our sandwiches by the loose chippings on the A597.

Vic's long-term manager and friend, Phil McIntyre, said:

Victoria has been a part of our lives as a friend, devoted mother and national treasure for thirty years. She was always modest, generous and undemanding. A super person and a super and unique talent. There will be an unfillable void left on all levels and we will miss her deeply.

Duncan Preston, who appeared alongside Victoria in many of her shows including *dinnerladies* and *As Seen On TV*, told the *Mirror* that she was a

champion of the common people.

Dinnerladies star Sue Devaney remembered her friend Victoria Wood when she told school leavers at Greenbank Preparatory School

it ain't what you do, it's the way that you do it.

The Rochdale born comedienne and musical theatre star was the special guest at the independent preparatory school's annual speech day, this year held in Screen 8 at the Parrswood cinema complex. Sue, who toured the world in the musical *Mamma Mia*, playing Rosie (the role) made famous by Julie Walters, and has just finished a run as Gracie Fields in a musical biography of the Lancashire lass, told the children about her chats with one of the all time greats of her profession Victoria Wood.

Vic would say to me, it's not all about education and qualifications, perhaps she was comforting me because unlike you or indeed her good self, I didn't really have any, but it's about enthusiasm, energy and the courage to do what you want to do. It was the best advice I ever had.

South Manchester News

Comedian Rhod Gilbert told BBC Radio Wales:

She was one of the greats... stand-up, sketch writer, musician. She was physically so funny, her eyes, her face, her comic timing, everything. She captured the mundane side of everyday life perfectly. She walks through a door at the back of a sketch and you're laughing already. She's the very definition of funny bones.

Actor and singer Michael Ball:

The most loyal and lovely friend you could ever wish for.

Victoria's friend and long-time comedy collaborator Julie Walters said:

Too heart sore to comment. The loss of her is incalculable.

Comedy actor Reece Sheersmith, who worked with Wood on BBC drama *Eric and Ernie* and other productions, tweeted:

RIP the brilliant Victoria Wood. She was such an inspiration - unparalleled comedy genius. What terrible shocking news.

Comedian and *Absolutely Fabulous* actress Jennifer Saunders tweeted:

Can't believe Vic has gone. She was truly an inspiration and had so much left to give and we won't see it. She was so funny. All of us bow down to Vic Wood. There will never be another. Fact. Vic was simply one of the funniest writers and performers this country has ever produced. She was an inspiration and will be terribly missed.

When Saunders later received the Award for Outstanding Contribution from *Glamour* magazine, she dedicated it to Victoria:

I dedicate this award to someone who passed away this year, Victoria Wood. She was a great friend to us and it was a great loss.

I've just had my TV mended. I say mended - a shifty young man in plimsolls waggled my aerial and wolfed my Gypsy Creams, but that's the comprehensive system for you. **(Kitty)**

Journalist and broadcaster Caitlin Moran tweeted:

Oh, Victoria Wood. You were so my hero. I can quote whole scripts by heart. Seeing Victoria Wood on TV - working-

class, silly, bookish, silly, clever, doing stand-up, singing, acting - made me think 'Girls can do this'.

Photographer and director Ben Lawrence told *The Telegraph*:

She made the mundane seem magical. Many comics attempt observational humour but no-one has made such a success of it as Victoria Wood. Razor-sharp, humane, and very, very funny, her gift was in finding humour in the everyday.

Also in *The Telegraph*, author Chrissy Iley wrote:

Wood's comedy usually has its basis in real, seemingly unimportant people. She's very relatable, and once won a poll of people you'd most like to live next door to.

Stand-up Sarah Millican tweeted:

So incredibly sad to hear that Victoria Wood has died. A true comedy icon.

John Cleese tweeted:

Shocked by news of Victoria Wood. I worked with her last year and was reminded of what a superlative performer she was. Only sixty-two!

Comedian Rory Bremner tweeted:

No. NO. This is too much. Now lovely, warm, funny, brilliantly talented Victoria Wood has gone. Words, songs, plays, she wrote the lot. So sad.

Great British Bake Off presenter and comedian Sue Perkins tweeted:

RIP, the brilliant, brilliant Victoria Wood.

Comedian Alan Carr tweeted:

Another legend gone.

Sir Lenny Henry said:

I am devastated - this is very, very sad news. Victoria will be sorely missed. Always funny, she worked incredibly hard. A killer stand-up and a fantastic songwriter.

Comedy actor Dawn French:

There will never be another.

Comedian Catherine Tate said:

It's so shocking and sad. We have lost an incredible talent who was a huge influence and inspiration to so many - a true game changer.

Comedian Ricky Gervais tweeted:

RIP the brilliant Victoria Wood. So innovative, funny and down to earth.

Bond actor Sir Roger Moore said:

Difficult to absorb the news about Victoria Wood. She was a total joy to work with and watch on TV.

Comic and author Mark Steel:

A brilliant amusing warm woman she was, that Victoria Wood.

Producer and director Geoff Posner told *The Telegraph*:

The world will truly be a poorer place without Victoria Wood. But, in the words of Mrs Overall, Never mind. Bingo Tuesday.

Comedy writer and actor Sanjeev Bhaskar:

I think Victoria Wood changed a fundamental attitude towards women and comedy in this country, as performer and writer.

Award-winning TV presenters Ant and Dec said:

Very sad to hear of the passing of Victoria Wood. Another great taken from us in 2016. RIP.

Eastenders actor Danny Dyer tweeted:

Victoria was my first major crush. A world without Victoria Wood is a sad sad thing. RIP beautiful. 2016... the year of taking the greats.

Great British Bake Off judge and baker Paul Hollywood, who worked with Victoria on a recent Comic Relief special of the show, tweeted:

A sad loss, I was fortunate to meet Victoria Wood a very funny, lovely lady.

Actor Richard Armitage tweeted:

RIP Victoria Wood. Hilarious northern Lass who gave many of her funniest lines away.

Sherlock star Mark Gatiss tweeted:

Inconceivable that Victoria Wood has gone. She had a kindly yet savage eye for the ordinariness and the grotesquerie of life.

Duncan Preston, who appeared alongside Victoria in her BBC sitcom *dinnerladies*, said:

I am shocked. All I know is it's a great loss to comedy in this country. She was a very special writer and the world has lost a great comedian.

Hello, I'm Kitty, I've had a boob off and I can't stomach whelks.

Singer Morrissey of indie rock band The Smiths wrote on his fan site True to You:

Tears today for my dear friend Victoria Wood. So unbearable that it cannot be true. I am lost. (Her comedy) was very, very revolutionary, not just for women but for men as well. They were completely different, very intelligent. It seemed to be a different kind of humour that hadn't been on television before. A different way of thinking, a different way of telling a joke and a different way of being silly. She was very unique.

Wendy Harmer of *The Australian* wrote:

She was a champion of the 'little woman'.

Bury Grammar School Girls, naturally proud of their star former pupil, announced:

We are deeply saddened to hear of the loss of one of our most famous and much loved former pupils. Her humour, warmth, intelligence and winning combination of self-confidence and self-deprecation have made her an inspiration to our students over the years. As a strong northern woman and fabulous role model, we will always be proud to count Victoria Wood as an old girl.

Writing in the *Methodist Recorder*, Norman Grigg said:

Any one of Victoria Wood's talents could have sustained a career, but she did it all with such modesty - 'giving all the best lines to others' as Julie Walters said - that maybe we didn't fully comprehend just how talented she was. Other actors) all agreed that when she died, her talent was far from spent and that she could well have become an Oscar winning screen writer.

Tributes came from fans:

Sarah Smith tweeted:

Just saw ITV's tribute to the gentle genius of #VictoriaWood. We laughed. We cried. We ate gipsy creams in our leg warmers.

Tributes were also paid across the Atlantic, with *Bridesmaids* and *Ghostbusters* director Paul Feig praising the comedian.

Victoria, nominated fourteen times won six BAFTAS for her performing, writing and acting, and was also honoured with a special BAFTA tribute in 2005. In the BAFTA awards ceremony shortly after her death, Victoria was the first to be shown in the 'those who have left us' spot. In her acceptance speech on receiving the best female performance in a comedy prize for her role in E4's *Chewing Gum*, her second BAFTA, Michaela Cole paid tribute:

I would like to pay my respects to Victoria Wood, with [this award] in my hand.

National newspapers published their obituaries and their appreciation for Victoria's work. *Guardian Opinion*:

'National Treasure' is an overused term. But the prime minister was right to use it about Victoria Wood, because it's exactly what she was. Wood combined Alan Bennett's ear for dialogue, Noël Coward's songwriting skills, Ronnie

Barker's comic acting talent and Ken Dodd's command of gag-cracking. She had the loveability of a Gracie Fields or an Eric Morecambe and at her best she could channel some of the same humanist poignancy as a Chaplin or a Chekhov. Let's be clear, though, what kind of 'National Treasure' Wood actually was. She died in London on Wednesday, but Wood was a northern, English, working-class, Lancastrian and Mancunian female treasure. She was the authentic voice of an optimistic, decent, unpretentious, take-people-as-they-come, mucking-in sort of Britishness that is almost always ignored when the posh and the populist try to define this country's virtues, but which still binds people together every bit as strongly as any monarch.

The *Mirror's* Carole Malone wrote:

Victoria Wood was seen as one of the foremost female comics Britain ever produced. No one had an inkling she was dying of cancer. She lived with it just like she had lived the rest of her life - in private and with dignity. To the end she was shy and northern and ordinary. Victoria Wood was content to let other people be the 'stars' even though many would never have been stars without her genius. She wrote her best lines for others. And no one could write comedy and pathos the way she did and cram both into a single sentence. Victoria Wood still has me smiling even as we say our last goodbye. 'Life's not fair,' she once said. 'Some of us drink champagne in the fast lane. Some of us eat sandwiches by the loose chippings on the A597'. Victoria could have afforded the champagne route, but you just know she'd have been happier in a deckchair on the edge of the A597. We loved and connected with her because of her observational skills of northern working-class life. And even though she was rich and famous and feted she never let it change who she was. I still can't believe she's gone. The only consolation is that she crammed so much comedy into her too short life that we'll be laughing with her for years to come.

Playwright Abi Morgan wrote in *The Observer*:

I loved Victoria Wood and the one time I got to meet her I fluffed it. She was calm and modest and the coolest point in the room. I talked bollocks. She was kind. In my mind, I rework the moment: I am plucking my favourite lines from her songs and she is gaily laughing; we might even become best friends. Because you wanted to know Victoria Wood. You wanted to know anyone who could rhyme 'this folly is jolly, bend me over backwards on the hostess trolley'. And I genuinely feel sad today. The brilliance of her writing as both a lyricist and dramatist stays with me. She sounded like the people I grew up with, went to school with. Except in her mouth the lines are funnier, warmer, delivered with such joie de vivre and mischievousness. 'Beat me on the bottom with a Woman's Weekly' *can still make my mother and I spontaneously laugh, even after all these years. For me,* Let's Do It! *will forever be the anthem of my teens'.*

I have a wardrobe full of brand new things because I wouldn't try them on in the shop.

The *Mirror*'s Simon Boyle reported that, in her last illness, Victoria had joked with another patient in hospital.

Victoria was the one joking around to disguise her own fears about another round of tests in her secret six-month battle with cancer. Tragically, the disease had already taken such a toll on her that her hospital companion didn't recognise the much-loved star of TV and stage, who died last week aged just sixty-two. Fellow patient Sue Spinks revealed how she met Victoria at the Finchley Memorial Hospital in north London a few weeks ago. She tells how the award-winning comedian, who entertained millions over three decades, was still able to laugh in the face of her disease and to make Sue smile. 'Victoria was on her own at the time, and just started chatting to me,' said Sue, sixty, from north London.

We were both waiting in a cafe area ahead of going in to see a doctor, and she was asking lots about me. But it wasn't until she got up and left that I even realised who she was. She looked so different. She had lost a lot of weight. I remembered her being a little chubby before, but she was very thin and her hair looked much darker. It was sad to see, but it obviously hadn't affected her sense of humour because she was still cracking jokes. There was some very bad weather at the time and she was joking about who gave the storms all those silly names. 'She was such a lovely lady and it's very sad news that she has passed away'.

Prior to her death, I was not told of Vic's terminal illness, although I guess that was just on a 'need to know' basis. All my adult life I have been in the public eye, at least in the North East, and ever since Vic came to the fore scarcely a week has gone by without someone from the media contacting me about Victoria. Vic very much wanted her illness to be kept secret to all but a small number. Clearly she or someone close to her thought that if I had been told about it, I might have inadvertently 'blabbed' to the press. Not that I would have done.

A source told the *Sunday Mirror* last week of plans for the funeral:

> She has always made it clear that she doesn't crave publicity or fanfare, and the expectation is that her funeral will be a very intimate affair.

Victoria's funeral was shrouded in the strictest secrecy, no doubt according to her wish.

The *Sun* was compelled to write:

> It is believed the Prestwich-born comedy legend was cremated at a ceremony in Golders Green, North London. Mourners included daughter Grace, 27, son Henry, 23 and former partner Geoffrey Durham. The ceremony was a short distance from her family home in Highgate, North London, where she lived out her final days.

> Comedy legend Victoria Wood was remembered with 'a strong element of humour' at her funeral on Wednesday. The comedy legend - who died last month aged sxty-two following a 'short but brave' battle with cancer - was laid to rest in an intimate and private service this week. According to the Sun,

> the star's family and friends made sure it was 'full of laughter' to honour the way the BAFTA award-winning comic brought joy to the lives of so many in her lifetime. A source said: 'It was a small and private affair, which is what Victoria wanted. The family were very conscious that they didn't want cameras. Julie [Walters] was one of her closest friends from the entertainment industry who attended. There was a strong element of humour as everyone knew that's what she wanted. She spent her life making people

laugh so a light-hearted and celebratory tone was appropriate. The service was full of laughter.

Naturally I would have liked to be at Victoria's funeral, but I wasn't invited. Whoever made that decision, I hold no grudge or resentment. Quite apart from my work as an Independent Celebrant, conducting non-religious weddings and funerals, I strongly hold the belief that no-one has the absolute 'right' to be at anybody's funeral, regardless of their relationship. Somebody didn't want me at the funeral - I don't need to know who it was - and I totally respect that.

But, along with a couple of hundred others, I was invited to Victoria's memorial service at St James's Church in London's Piccadilly on July 4th 2016. This was a most joyous occasion, a truly uplifting and moving celebration of Victoria's life. The highlight for me was to see and hear my opera singer niece Grace Durham, Vic's daughter, sing a J S Bach cantata accompanied by pianist Timothy Ravalde. The whole event was superbly produced as professionally as any West End show, with Adele Fowler of the Phil McIntyre organisation at the heart of the proceedings.

The Revd Lucy Winkett, Rector of St James's, gave the welcome and the blessing and said prayers. There were tributes from Jane Wymark, Harriet Thorpe, Daniel Rigby, Julie Walters and Lesley Schatzberger. Piers Wenger read a poem by William Wordsworth. There were two of Victoria's songs from Ria Jones (*Fourteen Again*) and Michael Ball (*Go With It*), accompanied by Nigel Lilley on the piano. The Royal Academy of Music Brass played before and after the service. There was a collection in aid of Jessie's Fund.

Jane Wymark said she had met Vic in 1971 in the Green Room

at the start of her second year at Birmingham University at nineteen years old. She read from a book by 'Miss Read', pen name of children's novelist Dora Jessie Saint. Harriet Thorpe and Victoria met via their children. They both went on a Breast Cancer Walk and sang World War One marching songs like *It's a Long, Long Way to Tipperary*, and *Pack up your Troubles in your Old Kit Bag and Smile, Smile, Smile*.

She [Victoria] made us get on with things, she made us smile all the time, said Wymark.

Piers Wenger gave a reading from *An Evening Walk* by Wordsworth who lived at Dove Cottage in the Lake District. Victoria bought nearby Swiss Cottage at Hawkshead and went on the same walk. Daniel Rigby, who in 2011 won a best actor BAFTA for his portrayal of the young Eric Morecambe in *Eric and Ernie*, with Victoria playing his mother, said that he had stayed in Vic's spare room for a year at her invitation.

Julie Walters gave an all-too-realistic portrayal of a demented am-dram theatre director from the sketch *Piecrust Players*, written by Vic for her TV show *VWASOTV* in 1985.

She was one of the best said Michael Ball.

Former Bury Grammar School Girls schoolmate Lesley Schatzberger, founder of Jessie's Fund, said:

We both felt like misfits.

She played clarinet alongside Victoria's trumpet in the Bury Military Band and school orchestra.

Performing at the Bush Theatre,* Wood and Walters *hung out of the window at lunchtimes, watching passers-by. Spotting Harold Pinter standing at the bus stop, Wood

shouted: 'You're a writer, we could do with one of those up here!'

Vic didn't want to write her own life story. In 2014 she told *Mail* journalist Richard Barber:

> If I ever did, I'd want it to be really, really good. Not, 'And then I did this and then I did that and then I met Julie Walters'. I'm not interested in explaining my memories to other people. My memories are filtered into my work.

That was typical Victoria. She always wanted her work to speak for itself. For her, fame and celebrity were not objectives in themselves, but confirmation that what she did was accepted and enjoyed. The fame (and the money - she was superb in matters of business) also enabled her to do the work she wanted, with the actors, directors and other professionals she wanted, and the clout to get the backing to move on to new fields of endeavour.

Victoria was always reluctant to talk about her private life, or to reveal her feelings. She always, always wanted her work to speak for itself. But, on rare occasions, she did reveal something of herself in interviews. Although she denied it, I'm sure that Vic didn't like press interviews. In 2011 Chrissy Iley of *The Telegraph* reported:

> I feel, in the first few minutes of talking to her, that I'm torturing her.

Vic replied:

> No, people always think I hate doing interviews. I don't. I wouldn't do them if I didn't like them. I have to say that at the start of every interview.

When Vic had a new show coming up, she would pick a particular newspaper, radio or TV station, and give them an interview. Obviously that was to promote her show: everybody does it. But in addition she would tell the world a little bit more about herself. This was almost the only time she would reveal herself to the world. That's why I've had to rely heavily on published interviews about details of her life and work in order to complete the picture. Vic never published her autobiography, nor was there any sign that she ever intended to do so. I feel very strongly that I owe it to the public, and particularly to Vic's legion of fans, to present as full a picture as I can.

In his appreciation of Victoria's life. Louis Barfe of the Express wrote:

> *Victoria had a brilliant ear and an unerring ability to make the mundane hilarious. Somehow, she managed to combine tremendous warmth and humanity with a sharp edge. Long after her untimely death last week at the age of just sixty-two, lines she wrote will pop into many people's minds daily, sometimes unaided, sometimes with a bit of help from life.*

> *An example: one Sunday last summer I was having lunch in a pub with various family members. I've never heard laughter like it. As the young waitress brought our starters, she said 'Two Soups?' The entire table, three generations aged from seven to their 60s, collapsed into fits of laughter. The waitress had to be reassured that she'd done nothing wrong, and that a visit to YouTube looking for Victoria Wood and Two Soups would explain everything.*

> *That sketch featuring Julie Walters as a deaf, doddery,*

waitress with Celia Imrie and Duncan Preston as diners in a hurry, has come to be regarded as a classic, but even on the night it was recorded it was clearly something very special. 'The audience reaction in the studio was immense. I've never heard laughter like it' recalls Roy Gould, later to direct hits such as You Rang M'Lord *and* Oh Doctor Beeching! *but then a production manager with the enviable job of running the studio floor.*

Vic said in the read-through that it looks rubbish on the page but just wait until Jules does it. Jules just marked it all week in rehearsals and then went for it on the recording. I actually bit into my bottom lip and drew blood to stop myself from corpsing. I was trying to keep out of Celia's eyeline as I could see her going.

As a performer Wood was always so gloriously vivacious but off-stage she was a very private person. Even though she never socialised in the hotel bar when on location, she was popular with the cast and crew. 'She was very shy,' says Gould, 'One night at the Strathallan Hotel, Birmingham, the others commented on this as we had a couple of guest actors. So I went up to her room, knocked, and talked her into coming down for an hour. She was a perfectionist and the others adored her'.

Barfe also wrote:

The comedian was shy and a very private person off-stage As an example of her shyness, only producer Geoff Posner saw her rehearse The Ballad of Barry and Freda, *the song best known to most people as* Let's Do It! *Everyone else saw it first on the dress run. On the recording, Posner asked for a second take. She demurred, explaining that they wouldn't laugh the second time. 'I squeezed her hand and asked if she was OK,' Gould recalls. 'She did the number again and the audience laughed even louder. We still used take one'.*

Viv Groscrop wrote:

People go on about what a brilliant working-class comic she was. But the truth was she wrote hundreds of sketches about every aspect of class that covered the whole spectrum. She basically did a one-woman Little Britain *for the best part of forty years. She did posh brilliantly herself and wrote posh beautifully.*

I don't take notes - I make most of it up.

The critic and writer Clive James said of Victoria:

As a TV dramatist alone, she is on a par with Alan Bennett, while as a creator of comedy programmes she changed the field for women and indeed for everybody, because very few of the men were trying hard enough as writers before she came on the scene and showed them what penetrating social humour should actually sound like.

In a letter to the *Guardian*, Canon Chris Chivers of Cambridge wrote:

She (Victoria) was to read at the thanksgiving service in Westminster Abbey for Dame Thora Hird from the dame's autobiography. First she had to walk up the steps from her seat into the sacrarium at the east end of the abbey with Alan Bennett, who was giving the address. Rehearsing her, as one of the priests on the staff - itself, ludicrously unnecessary - I ventured to suggest that she needed to personalise her presence and the reading by introducing it. 'I don't want to get in the way', she responded 'But it will make the whole service if you inject something of yourself,' I implored her. She remained unconvinced. But on the day she began,

I was just thinking when I came up those steps with Alan ... we could really have come up in a stairlift'. The abbey erupted with joyous laughter as it recalled Dame Thora advertising such lifts. What a git to make people laugh with so few words. What a loss as one national treasure now joins another via the heavenly stairlift.

In a letter to the *Guardian*, Michael Byne wrote:

Surely I cannot be the only one to demand that Victoria Wood be given a state funeral. Maggie Thatcher was granted one for destroying our society. Victoria added to our sense of wellbeing and humanity.

In his Guardian column, Clive James wrote:

Victoria could fill the Albert Hall just by singing songs she wrote, but her central power was an infallible ear for the nuances of the national language.

Esther Rantzen told BBC Breakfast that Victoria should have been made a dame:

The thing about her humour was that even though it was very sharp, very clear-eyed, it was never cruel. She was never obscene, even though she was mischievous.

The *Mail* reported that when Victoria was asked how she felt about the prospect of becoming a dame, she said:

I don't want to be. It would depend on what my children wanted really. 'It doesn't matter to me one way or the other, but it might matter to them. So, if I were asked if I'd like a damehood, that's the recognition. 'If the kids said, 'Oh, Mum, that's so embarrassing, then I'd turn it down. On the other hand, if they really wanted me to have it, then I'd say yes.

Actor and television presenter Phillip Schofield said on air that Victoria generously lent his wife rent money when she was young and in need of help.

She was such a generous lady.

The *Mail*'s Richard Barber asked:

So, who was the real Victoria Wood? Well, first and foremost, she was a homebird who loved her two children, Grace, twenty-seven, and Henry, twenty-four, more than life itself. She'd have liked more, she once told me. And she couldn't wait to be a granny. 'But my kids are still a bit young for that yet. Mind you,' she joked, 'I'd have been perfectly happy if Grace had had a teenage pregnancy but she let me down badly. No thought for her mother.' She certainly gave them her full attention as they were growing up, just like any other mother. 'If I went around being Victoria Wood at home,' she said, 'we might be in trouble. But I close the front door and, to the children, I'm just Mum, plain and simple. I like to be normal.

For all that, her work ran motherhood a close second. 'You're fortunate if you have a job you like. In my job there's a huge amount of variety and camaraderie and gossip and excitement. Noël Coward once said that work was more fun than fun. I'd go along with that. 'And there's still so much more I want to do. I have ideas pinned to the notice board in my office at home. They can remain there for ages.'

Am I still driven? I suppose so, although it's more to do with the work than the fame or the money. Work isn't so much central to my life, as crucial.' Her marriage to magician Geoffrey Durham collapsed when he walked out of their home in Highgate, north London, in 2002. Work was her saviour. *'It's what I spend most of my time doing, and a lot of me goes into my work, so yes, it probably defines me.'*

In December 2015 Victoria starred alongside Timothy Spall in a Sky adaptation of *Fungus the Bogeyman*, saying in an interview at the time:

It's more to do with the work than the exposure, the fame or the money. Work is crucial to my life. My creativity is what defines me. I feel I can work as hard as I ever did.

Sadly, my sister Victoria died four months later at the age of sixty-two. How much more she could and would have done if she had lived?

The *Mirror*'s Sophie Malcolm and Neela Debnath revealed that Vic was working on a film when she died, 'a non-musical but a comedy'. I know from what Vic told me herself that she always wanted to write and produce a major film for the cinema. Sadly, it was not to be.

All I have ever wanted to do is make people laugh

CHAPTER TWELVE

VICTORIA'S STATUE

For some time after my sister Victoria died, I thought about what I could do to honour her memory and give my own personal tribute to this amazing woman who achieved so much after an unhappy childhood and years of struggle. Writing this book is an obvious way of doing just that. After all, I am first and foremost a writer. Three women I loved dearly have had perhaps the most influence on my life - my mother Nellie, my wife Frances and my sister Victoria - and I have now written biographies of all three.

I was proud and pleased to be asked to take part in a Victoria Wood Tribute *Beat Me on the Bottom with a* Woman's Weekly at the Strutts Centre, Belper in Derbyshire in July 2016, profits to Cancer Research. This event - with me playing just a small part - was a great success. So much so, that I have been asked to be MC for another Tribute Evening at the Belper Festival in May 2017. I must acknowledge the great work done by all the talented volunteers who took part and particularly George Gunby, the man behind these two evenings and indeed the Festival as a whole. As enjoyable as these events are, they are but passing moments.

I still felt that Victoria should have a permanent memorial, something the public would recognise and which Vic's many, many fans (for they are legend!) could visit and feel a close connection with her. When Victoria Railway Station Manches-

" We are NOT amused "

ter (where you can still catch a train to Bury) was renamed Victoria Wood Station for an hour in June 2016, I thought it would be great if the change was made permanent. After all, Liverpool has John Lennon airport, New York John F Kennedy airport and so on.

Victoria Wood Station could have been the home of a museum and archive dedicated to her, with videos of her work available to watch at any time. But my suggestion fell on deaf ears. 'It takes two to tango' and without widespread support from local office holders as well as the people themselves, there's no point in me expending energy on a lost cause.

So you can imagine my great joy when I was told by the *Bury Times* that members of Bury Council, including the leader(!) were talking about a memorial statue of Victoria. The problem is, in these times of austerity and budget cuts, the Council simply cannot pay for something like this. They mentioned Crowdfunding, but really it would be better for such an appeal (à la mode) to come from an individual rather than an official body like the Council. So, I took up the baton, and ran with it.

This time my outstretched hand of friendship and support was warmly grasped and firmly shaken. As a local councillor myself for forty years and indeed a Council Leader for six, you can imagine I am all too familiar with red tape, obstructions and objections of all kinds. How wonderful to have a positive response! I immediately set up my Crowdfunding appeal through the JustGiving site, asking the Great British Public (otherwise known as Victoria Wood fans) to donate £20,000, (later raised to £30,000, with Dame Judi Dench giving £1,000). £4,000 came in the first week! I then met with Bury Council Leader Rishi Shori and Tony Trehy, the Council's Arts and Museums manager.

Our agreement in essence was that I would raise the funds and the Council would provide the site and maintain the statue thereafter. With a fair wind, we hoped to have the finished statue in place by May/June 2017.

While I am open minded about the exact form of the statue, I have very firm ideas about the type of permanent monument it should be. What I have in mind is something on the lines of the bronze statue of Eric Morecambe, which has pride of place on the seafront in his home town (of Morecambe, of course!) The much-loved comedian is shown in typical pose. This is just what people today want - it's all about the selfie! Fans love to have their photographs taken alongside their heroes.

So Victoria's statue has to be lifesize and lifelike, and in a typical and recognisable pose. Vic at the piano had to be ruled out due to the cost of casting a solid bronze piano being more than the statue itself. In a public on-line poll run by Bury Council, Vic's fans voted 60% for 'Bren' from *dinnerladies* in her canteen smock, and 40% for 'Kimberley's Friend' in mac and beret, so 'Bren' it is.

The position of the statue is equally important - it must be in the town centre and in suitable surroundings: Eric Morecambe's statue certainly ticks these boxes. I say this because I am disappointed with the siting - not the statue itself - of Stan Laurel in Bishop Auckland, where I lived for over forty years. Unfortunately the Laurel statue has been placed with its back to and just a couple of feet from a very busy road. In my view this spoils the 'selfie'. Laurel could so easily have been placed in a much better position a few yards away, but then I wasn't in charge of that job.

But when Messrs Shori and Trehy took me to the Library Gardens in the centre of Bury, I could see straight away that this was an ideal position. It is in a flower garden, close to the bus station, museum and library.

If when you read this my Crowdfunding appeal is still in being, please do contribute what you can. You will have the satisfaction of helping bring about a very suitable, permanent memorial to one of the very brightest talents of our generation. If you do give or have already given, I thank you most warmly.

To contribute on line to the *Let's Do It!* Victoria Wood Memorial Appeal, log on to either

tinyurl.com/letsdoitforvictoria or crowdfunding.justgiving.com/chris-footewood

And thank you

Chris Foote Wood

Victoria as 'Bren' from dinnerladies
(Image supplied by BBC).

" I'm looking for my fwend.. 'ave you seen 'er ?"

BAFTAS AND OTHER AWARDS

Victoria Wood and her programmes won so many BAFTA (British Academy of Film and Television Arts) awards that on one award night top TV presenters Ant and Dec thanked Vic for 'not doing a series this year'. In all Vic won six individual BAFTAS, plus one Special Award. In addition, her programmes - in which she was often writer and producer as well as actor/performer - won no fewer than twelve BAFTAS, making nineteen in all. She was individually nominated twelve times.

Victoria's BAFTA role of honour (* individual awards) reads:

1986 Best Light Entertainment Programme *VWASOTV*, Geoff Posner director

* 1986 Best Light Entertainment Performance *WVASOTV*

1987 Best Light Entertainment Programme *VWASOTV*, Geoff Posner director

* 1987 Best Light Entertainment Performance *WVASOTV* (BAFTA also for Julie Walters)

1988 Best Light Entertainment Programme *VWASOTV*, Geoff Posner director

1989 Best Light Entertainment Programme *An Audience With Victoria Wood*, David G Hillier director, producer

* 1989 Best Light Entertainment Performance *An Audience With Victoria Wood*

1990 Best Light Entertainment Programme *Victoria Wood*, Victoria Wood writer/producer, Geoff Posner director, Kevin Bishop producer

* 1990 Best Light Entertainment Performance *Victoria Wood*

1995 Best Single Drama *Pat and Margaret*, Ruth Caleb producer, Gavin Millar director, Victoria Wood writer/producer

* 1995 Best Light Entertainment Performance *Victoria Wood: Live In Your Own Home*

1995 Best Actress *Pat and Margaret*

1999 Best Comedy Programme or Series *dinnerladies*, Geoff Posner director & producer, Victoria Wood writer/producer

2000 Best Situation Comedy *dinnerladies*, Geoff Posner director & producer, Victoria Wood writer/producer

2001 Best Comedy Programme or Series *Victoria Wood With All The Trimmings*, Jemma Rodgers producer, John Birkin director, Victoria Wood writer/producer

* 2005 Special Award (tribute)

2007 Best Single Drama *Housewife, 49*

* 2007 Best Actress *Housewife, 49*

2011 Best Single Drama *Eric and Ernie*

Other achievements and awards won by Victoria and her programmes:

1978 Vic's stage play *Talent* wins Plays and Players award and she gets the Evening Standard Most Promising Playwright award

1979 Vic wins Most Promising Writer award (Pye Television) for her play *Talent*

1986 November 29th Victoria stars in the *Royal Variety Show*

1986 *Victoria Wood: As Seen On TV* wins Broadcasting Guild Award, best light entertainment show

1987 Named BBC Personality of the Year by the Variety Club of Great Britain

1988 Wins *TV Times Readers Award* for Funniest Woman

1991 August Victoria makes her pop debut with her song *Smile Song* for Comic Relief b/w *Stonk* by Hale & Pace tops the pop singles charts

1992 December *Victoria Wood's All Day Breakfast* (BBC TV Christmas Day Special) wins Writers Guild Award for Best Light Entertainment Programme

1994 Film screenplay *Pat and Margaret* BBC1 Screen One Autumn Season wins Broadcasting Press Guild Award for best single drama, Vic wins Best Actress Award; *Pat and Margaret* also wins Best Actress and Best Screenplay at Rheims TV Festival

1995 Wins Best Female Comedy Performance, British Comedy Awards

1997 Awarded OBE, Queen's Birthday honours

1998 November *dinnerladies* (first series, six episodes) BBC1 wins Press Prize at Montreux Festival.

1999 November *dinnerladies* (second series) BBC1 wins Best New TV Comedy at the National Television Awards

2000 *dinnerladies* wins Best TV Comedy, British Comedy Awards, and Writer of the Year Award

2001 May Victoria awarded Best Live Stand Up at the British Comedy Awards

2008 awarded CBE, Queen's Birthday Honours

2011 Women in Film and Television, Lifetime Achievement Award

2015 Wins Comic Relief Bakeoff

REFERENCES

Books

Daily Journal, Stanley Wood 1944-1988

Nellie's Book, Helen Wood and Chris Foote Wood, Sutton Publishing/History Press 2006

The Swish of the Curtain, Pamela Brown, Hodder Modern Classics 1941

The Funny Side of Victoria Wood, Bruce Dessau, Orion Media 1997

Victoria Wood: The Biography, Neil Brandwood, Virgin Books 2006

Newspapers/Magazines

Daily Telegraph, Charles Spencer 1990, 2001, 2009, Jasper Rees 2001, Chrissy Iley 2011, 2012, Ben Lawrence 2012, Serena Davis 2013, Tim Martin 2014, Benji Wilson 2015, Geoff Posner 2016, Ben Lawrence 2016

The Guardian, Decca Aitkenhead 2010, Stuart Jeffries 2016, Ian Jack 2016, Clive James 2016, Canon Chris Chivers 2016, Michael Byrne 2016 *Daily Mail*, Frances Hardy 2009, Richard Barber, 2014, 2016, Paul Allen 2011, Esther Rantzen 2016, Philip Schofield 2016

Daily Express, Maureen Paton 1985, Louis Barfe 2016, Neela Debnath 2016

The Independent, Rachel Halliburton 2002, 2007

The Times 1982

Daily Mirror, Hilary Bonner 1986, Carole Malone 2016, Fiona

Phillips 2016, Simon Boyle 2016, Sophie Malcom 2016

The Observer, Richard Brooks, Abi Morgan 2016

The Australian, Wendy Harmer 2016

The Sun 2016, Duncan Preston 2016

The Guardian, Lucy Mangan 2016, Michael Byrne 2016

Sunday Times 1982

Sunday Mirror 2016

Sunday Post 1986

Daily Mail, Nigel Dempster 1989, Frances Hardy 2009

Mail on *Sun*day, Angela Levin 1993, Chris Hastings 2016

Radio Times 1986, Esther Rantzen 2016

TV Quick 1991

The Listener 1980

Manchester Evening News 1986, 2016

Lancashire Evening Post 1980

South Manchester News 2016

Stoke Sentinel 2016

Northants Post, Steve Mills 2016

Vogue 1980

Time Out 1985

OK Magazine 1996

Cosmopolitan 1982

Methodist Recorder 2016

The Stage 1985, Neil Bonner 2016

Best Magazine 1990

Woman's Own, Jo Weedon 1987

Woman's Realm 1977

Television

New Faces 1974

Summer Show 1975

Clive James 1990

Gloria Hunniford, *Wogan* 1991

BAFTA award ceremony 2016

BBC TV news 2016

Radio

BBC Radio 4 *Desert Island Discs* 03.02.1987 Michael Parkinson

BBC Radio 4 *Desert Island Discs* 22.12.2007 Kirsty Young

BBC Radio Wales Rhod Gilbert 2016

Internet

BBC2 online interview 2014; Richard E Grant interview 2016; Vic Groskop, Jude Kelly, Duncan Preston, Stuart McFarlane, Applecake, Isolde 2, Reece Sheersmith, Jennifer Saunders, Caitlin Moran, Sarah Millican, John Cleese, Rory Bremner, Sue Perkins, Alan Carr, Sir Lenny Henry, Dawn French, Catherine Tate, Ricky Gervais, Sir Roger Moore, Mark Steel, Phil McIntyre, Sanjeev Baskar, Ant and Dec, Danny Dwyer, Paul Hollywood, Richard Armitage, Mark Gattis, Morrisey (all 2016), Paul Feig, Sarah Sith, Weight Loss Resources, Wikipedia

Victoria Wood: Books

Lucky Bag, the Victoria Wood Song Book, Methuen 1984

Up To You, Porky! (sketches) Methuen 1985

Barmy (sketches featuring *Acorn Antiques*), Methuen 1987

Victoria Wood Plays 1 (three plays), Methuen 1988

Mens Sana in Thingummy Doodah (six plays), Methuen 1990

Pat & Margaret (film script), Methuen 1994

Chunky, the Victoria Wood Omnibus, Methuen 1996

dinnerladies, first helpings (six episodes), Methuen 1999

Victoria's Empire, Hodder & Staunton 2007

Victoria Wood: Television

Talent TV play, Granada 1979

Nearly a Happy Ending, TV play, Granada 1980

Happy Since I Met you, TV play Granada 1981

An Audience With...Victoria Wood, LWT TV show 1988

Pat and Margaret, BBC1 TV film 1994

Victoria's Big Fat Documentary, BBC1 TV documentary 2004

Housewife, 49, BBC1 TV film 2006

Eric and Ernie, TV film BBC2 2011

Loving Mrs Hatto, TV film 2012

Victoria Wood's Nice Cup of Tea, BBC1 TV documentary 2013

That Day We Sang, BBC2 TV film 2014

Also, Victoria's TV sketch shows, sitcoms etc

VICTORIA WOOD TIMELINE

1953 May 19th Victoria Wood born at Prestwich, Bury, Greater Manchester

1966 August Wood family holiday Dover Liege Aaachen Frankfurt

1967 Sat Dec 17th BBC Radio Afternoon Theatre *Call Corporal Watson* (by Stanley Wood)

1968 Wed-Sat July 9-12th Vicky's Stratford trip

1969 Wed-Fri October 1-3rd Vicky at Stratford

1969 November 3rd Stan meets Peter Eckersley (producer)

1969 Dec 16/17th *The Winter's Tale* BGS Girls Roger Kay Hall Vic plays Autolycus (a rogue) and is one of seven girls credited with composing the music

1971-74 Vic takes drama degree at Birmingham University

1972 Mon May 29th *Coronation Street* (Stan)

1972 Wed September 20th *Coronation Street* (Stan)

1973 Tues June 5th Stan meets Phil McIntyre (agent)

1973 Birmingham University Department of Drama and Theatre Arts presents *The Way of the World*. Stage Manager: Victoria Wood

1974-78 Vicky works 'on and off' at folk clubs and late night theatres

1974 Sun September 15th Vicky on ITV

1974 Sat October 12th *New Faces* Vic is heat winner

1975 August 9 *Summer Show* (New Faces) ATV sketch show.

Marti Caine (singer/comedienne), Trevor Chance (singer), Aidan J Harvey (impressionist, winner, all winners show July 1974), Lennie Henry (sixteen years, impressionist), Charlie James (girl singer), Nicky Martin (compere/comedian, winner, all winners gala final), Victoria Wood (songwriter/comedienne)

1975 Edinburgh Festival *G.R.I.M.M.S* revue with Roger McGough

1975 Hampstead Theatre *G.R.I.M.M.S* revue with Roger McGough

1976 Vic still in Birmingham

1976 Mon May 10th Victoria on TV *A Camera and a Song*

1976 *That's Life* Vic takes over as resident songwriter from Jake Thackray

1976 Edinburgh Festival *Wordplay* revue with Roger McGough

1976 Hampstead Theatre *Wordplay* revue with Roger McGough

1976 Vic supports Jasper Carrott in his sell-out tour

1976 Vic meets Geoffrey Durham (four years younger) both struggling actors: it's 'love at first sight'. They marry in 1980

1976 Sat November 13th Victoria performs at Leicester, Phoenix Theatre

1977-82 Stage show: *Funny Turns* revue, Vic with husband Geoffrey Durham

1977 Victoria at 12 Oxford Street, Morecambe

1977 *Tickling My Ivories - An Evening with Victoria Wood* self-promoted

1978 *In at the Death* Bush Theatre, London, Vic in revue with Julie Walters (they bond instantly); Vic co-writes & appears in a sketch. Vic writes song *Love Song*

1978 Vic's play *Talent* wins Plays and Players award and Evening Standard Most Promising Playwright Award, Crucible Studio Theatre Sheffield transferrs to London ICA 1979

1979 Sun August 5th *Talent* TV play with Julie Walters, most promising writer award (Pye Television)

1980 Sat January 5th Vicky buys car Fiat 3-door hatchback 1300cc £2,500 MCK 146T

1980 Vic and Geoff still at 12 Oxford Street Morecambe

1980 June *Nearly a Happy Ending* TV play with music Granada Television (sequel to *Talent*)

1980 Stage musical *Good Fun* Crucible Theatre, Sheffield June 25 - July 12 with Polly James, Sam Kelly, Gregory Floy, Sue Wallace, Joe Figg, Meg Johnson, Noreen Kershaw, Christopher Hancock. 8-piece band. Original production directed by David Leland. Revival directed by David Firman. Vic writes song *I've Had It Up to Here*

1980 March 1st Victoria marries Geoffrey Durham at Lancaster register office

1981 Victoria and Geoff move to 22 Stankelt Road Silverdale near Carnforth in Lancashire, later moving to Cove Lea, also in Silverdale

1981 *Talent* stage play The Duke's Playhouse Lancaster June 10 - July 4th with Lesley Nightingale, Christine Moore, Nick Maloney, David Boyce, Reg Stewart, Matthew Marsh (not

Victoria)

1981 Sun August 9th *Happy Since I Met You* 3rd TV play for Granada Television 9.30pm Vic not in it, writes song *Living Together*

1981 *Wood and Walters* first TV sketch show with Granada Television: Vic insists in equal billing for her and co-star Julie Walters

1981 August 30th Octagon Theatre Bolton *Funny Turns* revue with Victoria and the Great Soprendo (husband Geoffrey Durham)

1982 Stage show *Funny Turns* at the King's Head in North London, then a West End season at the Duchess Theatre, Vic writes song *Thinking of You*

1982 Vic plays King's Head Pub Theatre for the first time

1983 Sat February 26th *Talent* at Chester Gateway Theatre

1983 Sun May 22nd Vicky on TV Channel 4

1983 Sun May 29th TV *Wood and Walters*

1983-84 Victoria's *Lucky Bag* tour (first of six stand-up shows)

1983 Sat Aug 3rd Vicky at The Royal, Enderby

1983 *Lucky Bag* LP record

1983 Fri/Sat December 16/17 Vicky still at The Royal, Enderby

1984 Vic at the King's Head 'a cramped fringe theatre in the back room of a pub in Islington'

1984 February 14th *Lucky Bag* transfers from King's Head to the Ambassadors

1984 December *Lucky Bag The Victoria Wood Song Book* from

her solo show

1985 Vic again at the King's Head, Islington

1985 March 20th Vic starts tour

1985 Walt Disney Productions/Cherry Lane Records CD *Return to Oz* with Nicol Williamson, Jean Marsh, Piper Laurie b/w *Nearly a Shambles*

1985 *Up To You, Porky! The Victoria Wood Sketch Book* (Lucky Bag, Oct 1983, *Wood and Walters*, Jan 1982) *Victoria Wood As Seen on TV*, Jan 1985). Vic dedicates the book 'To Peter Eckersley, who liked a laugh'

1985 January *Victoria Wood As Seen On* TV (1st series) BBC2 with *Acorn Antiques*

1986 April 15th Victoria's one-woman show Preston Guild Hall, one of twenty-two dates

1986 November 10 Vic on front cover of *Radio Times*

1986 November *Victoria Wood As Seen On* TV (2nd series) BBC2 wins BAFTA Best Light Entertainment Programme

1986 November 29th Victoria stars in the *Royal Variety Show*

1986 Two BAFTAS for sketch show *Victoria Wood: As Seen On TV*, also wins Broadcasting Press Guild Award, best light entertainment show; BAFTA for Best Light Entertainment Programme and Best Light Entertainment Performance

1987 Feb 3rd BBC Radio 4 *Desert Island Discs* with Michael Parkinson

1987 Second series *VWASOTV* wins BAFTA Best Light Entertainment Programme

1987 October *Barmy - Victoria Wood Sketch Book* featuring *Acorn Antiques* episodes 1-12

1987 Autumn *Acorn Antiques Special* BBC2

1987 Autumn Tour inc Dublin, Belfast, ten nights London Palladium Oct 12-16 & Oct 21-23. Co-promoter Preston impresario Phil McIntyre, ends November; Victoria advertises the 'Pioneer Six' CD multiplayer

1987 Sketch show *Victoria Wood On* TV - *The Special* wins BAFTA for Best Light Entertainment Performance

1987 *BBC Personality of the Year* by the Variety Club of Great Britain.

1987 London Palladium sell-out run of solo stand-up

1988 Wins BAFTA for sketch show *Victoria Wood: As Seen On TV*

1988 Friday June 10th *An Audience With Victoria Wood* LWT 60-minute special. Wins BAFTAS for Best Light Entertainment Programme and Best Light Entertainment Performance

1988 Sun May 8th Vicky at Halifax

1988 Mon August 8th *The Mouse's Tale* BBC 1 4.35 starring Victoria Wood

1988 Wins *TV Times Readers Award for Funniest Woman*

1988 Best-selling Comedy Album *Victoria Wood - Live*

1989 Mon February 20th BBC *Jackanory* Vicky

1989 Sat May 13th BBC repeat 9.25 10.05

1989 Victoria Wood six individual half hour TV plays BBC

1989 Sat July 1st new piano Yamaha 77

1989 Sat July 15th Vicky and Geoff at Silverdale

1989 *Sun* November 16th Vicky 8.30 to 9pm

1989 Sat December 23rd Radio 4 Vic reads a Fairy Story

1990 Victoria and Geoff rent London flat, 106 Castillian Mansions W9 1HB

1990 Victoria and Geoff move to Cove Lea, Silverdale

1990 February *Money Well Spent* Comic Relief documentary, Ethiopia

1990 Mon May 21st-26th Victoria at the Opera House

1990 Thurs July 19th Vic's last show at end of tour

1990 September Book *Mens Sana in Thingummy Doodah and other nuggets of homely fun* (her six TV plays) published

1990 October Stage show *Victoria Wood Up West* sixty dates in ten weeks at the Strand Theatre followed by six week sell-out tour

1991 March Sell-out tour six weeks. Wins Best Stand-Up Comedy Performance, British Comedy Awards

1991 Sat March 16th Vic's last show, Bradford

1991 Thurs-Sat March 20-23 Vic in Bournemouth

1991 Wed June 12th Vicky Radio 2

1991 August Vic make charity single with *Smile Song* for Comic Relief, her pop debut, tops charts

1991 August 12th Vic and Geoff move to 7 Lampard House, 8 Maida Avenue, London. W2 1SS

1991 Best-selling live performance video *Victoria Wood - Sold*

Out

1991 Mon September 16th Vick on *Wogan*

1991 Wed November 6th Vicky 12.20 BBC1 *Pebble Mill* comedy

1991 November 2-8 VW on front cover of *TV Quick* 'Victoria Wood laughs her way around Britain'. Has been to Morecambe, Solihull, Derby - heading for Pebble Mill on Wednesday (Nov 6). St Austell, Glasgow, Harrogate, Sheffield, Nottingham, Melton Mowbray, London

1992 Fri January 17th Vicky's re-run BBC

1992 January 22nd Vic and Geoff move to Highgate, North London (Vic's final home)

1992 Fri January 24th Vicky 9pm BBC 2

1992 Friday February 7th Vicky 9pm BBC2

1992 Fri Feb 21st Vicky 9pm

1992 Mon September 21st Emily Wood is born (Chris's granddaughter, Vic's great-niece), later becomes stand-up comic, actor, model and presenter.

1992 December *Victoria Wood's All Day Breakfast* BBC TV Christmas Day Special. Wins Writers Guild Award Best Light Entertainment Programme

1992 Wed December 16th *Coronation Street* (Stan)

1993 *Victoria Wood* six month sell-out tour April-November Phil McIntyre presents

Sheffield City Hall, including fifteen-night sell-out run at the Albert Hall; Mon April 19 - Thurs Apr 22 (four nights)

Birmingham Symphony Hall; *Sun* Apr 25 - Wed Apr 28 (sold out) Extra dates Mon May 24 - Thurs May 27 (eight dates) Plymouth Pavilions; Mon May 3 - Thurs May 6 (four nights) Bristol Hippodrome; Mon May 10 - Thurs May 13 (four nights) Nottingham Royal Centre

Mon May 17 - Thurs May 20 (sold out) Tues Oct 12 - Fri Oct 15 (eight nights) Manchester Free Trade Hall; Mon May 31 - Thurs June 3 Extra dates: Mon June 7 & Tues June 8 (six dates) Leicester De Montfort Hall; Mon June 14 - Thurs June 17 (four nights) Liverpool Empire; Mon Jun 21 - Thurs June twenty-four extra dates: Mon June 28 - Thurs July 1 (eight dates) London The Royal Albert Hall; Tues Sept 21 -Sun Sept 26 (six dates) Bournemouth International Centre; Mon Oct 18 & Tues Oct 19 (two nights) Oxford Apollo; Mon Oct 25 - Thurs Oct 28 (four nights) Southampton Mayflower; Mon Nov 1 - Thurs Nov 4 (four nights) Newcastle City Hall; Mon Nov 15 & Tues Nov 16 (two nights) (thirteen venues, sixty dates)

1993 Victoria on front cover of *You* magazine (*Mail on Sunday*) June 27th *Tricky Vicky, an audience with the Queen of Comedy*: Angela Levin

1994 December *Victoria Wood Live in Your Own Home* BBC1, video of tour

1994 Film screenplay *Pat and Margaret* BBC1 Screen One Autumn Season. Wins Broadcasting Press Guild Award for best single drama; Best Actress; also wins Best Actress and best Screenplay at Rheims TV Festival

1994 Book *Pat and Margaret* (script)

1994 *Victoria Wood's Christmas Special* BBC1 based on stage show

1995 Comic Relief Zimbabwe for Red Nose Day stays with a farming family

1995 *Crewe to Crewe* BBC1 TV Great Railway Journeys of the World (1 ep)

1995 Wins Best Female Comedy Performance, British Comedy Awards.

1996 Cassette *Victoria Wood Encore*

1996 April UK tour new stage show, again culminating in fifteen sell-out nights at Royal Albert Hall

1996 *South Bank Show* documentary of tour and interview with Melvyn Bragg

1996 September Book *Chunky* omnibus published

1997 Sell-out run with stage show, Australia and New Zealand

1997 Awarded OBE Queen's Birthday honours

1997 *The Wind in the Willows* as the Tea Lady, Terry Jones film

1997 Video cassette *Victoria Wood Live* recorded show released

1997 CD *Real Life* collection of Victoria's songs

1998 January Book *Plays Vol 1*

1998 November *dinnerladies* (first series, six episodes) BBC1. Wins Press Prize at Montreux Festival. Victoria is also producer, all sixteen episodes, two series

1999 November *dinnerladies* (second series) BBC1. Wins Best New TV Comedy National Television Awards 1999

1999 Christmas Video *dinnerladies*

1999 Book *dinnerladies* first helpings' (six episodes)

1999 Christmas release Video cassette *dinnerladies 1*

2000 *dinnerladies* wins Best TV Comedy, British Comedy Awards 2000, and Writer of the Year Award

2000 Christmas Special *Victoria Wood with all the Trimmings* BBC BAFTA nominated Best Comedy Programme

2001 Victoria has emergency hysterectomy

2001 May Victoria takes on her first UK tour since 1997 and is awarded Best Live Stand Up at the British Comedy Awards

2001 Tour *Victoria Wood - At It Again* Phil McIntyre & Paul Roberts promoters (Albert Hall starts Wed Sept 19 2001): Reading The Hexagon *Sun* May 6; Milton Keynes The Stables *Sun* May 13; Northampton Derngate Tues May 15; Wellingborough The Castle *Sun* May 27; Watford The Colosseum Thurs June 14 *Sun* Jun 17; Folkestone Lees Cliff Hall Mon June 25;

Swindon Wyvern Theatre Tues June 26; Bristol Hippodrome Wed June 27 - Sat June 30 (four nights); Wolverhampton Civic Hall Mon July 2 - Thurs July 4 (three nights); Blackpool Opera House Fri July 6 Sat July 7; Manchester Palace Mon July 9 - Sat July 14 (six nights); Liverpool Empire Wed July 18 - Fri July 20 (three nights); Plymouth Pavilions Turs Sept 4 Wed Sept 5;

Oxford Apollo Thurs Sept 6 Fri Sept 7; Nottingham Royal Centre Wed Sept 12 - Fri Sept 14 (three nights); London Royal Albert Hall Wed Sept 19 - Fri Sept 21 Mon Sept 24 - Wed Sept 26 (six nights); Sheffield City Hall Mon Oct 8 - Wed Oct 10 (three nights); Bournemouth BIC Fri Oct 12;

Southend Cliffs Pavilion Mon Oct 15 Tues Oct 16; (nineteen

venues, forty-two dates)

2002 Vic and Geoff separate and later divorce

2003 April CD *Favourite Funny Women*

2004 *Victoria Wood's Big Fat Documentary* TV mini series (two progs) with Rosemary Conley, Michelle Csitos, Anne Diamond, Andrew Dunn, Vanesa Feltz, Sarah Ferguson, Nick Holder, Nigel Lawson

2005 *Acorn Antiques* stage musical, Theatre Royal, Haymarket

2005 special BAFTA tribute

2006 *Housewife, 49* ITV two BAFTAS for writing and acting

2007 Book *Victoria's Empire*

2007 CD *An Audience With Victoria Wood*

2007 May Book *Good Fun & Talent*

2007 Cassette *dinnerladies 2*

2007 Travel documentary *Victoria's Empire* (three progs) & BBC audio book. 1. Calcutta India, Hong Kong, Borneo 2. Ghana, Jamaica, Newfoundland 3. New Zealand, Australia, Zambia, finishing at the Victoria Falls

2007 Dec 22nd BBC Radio 4 *Desert Island Discs* with Kirsty Young

2007 Boxing Day Vic appears as 'Nana' in Granada's adaption of the Noel Streatfeild novel *Ballet Shoes*

2008 April CD *Victoria's Empire*

2008 awarded CBE in Queen's Birthday Honours

2009 BBC TV Victoria's Christmas Special demoted from

promised primetime Christmas Day slot without telling her

2010 TV film *Eric and Ernie*: Vic plays Mrs Bartholomew Ernie's mother)

2011 Vic plays Granny Driver in TV movie *The Borrowers*

2011 *Great Railway Journeys* (BBC) *Crewe to Crewe*

2012 DVD CD *Victoria Wood Live*

2013 *Victoria Wood's Nice Cup of Tea* BBC two part special with Morrisey

2013 *Housewife, 49* stage version

2015 Wins *Comic Relief Bakeoff*

2015 Christmas in *Fungus the Bogeyman* with Timothy Spall Sky TV (voice only)

2016 April 20th Victoria Wood dies at her Highgate home

ABOUT THE AUTHOR

What's this? (I hear you say) 'an Author writing his own 'About the Author'? What is the world coming to?' Well, as the 'About the Author' feature is almost always written by the Author him/herself, why not admit it? It is a bit egotistical writing about yourself in the third person, pretending to be some sort of impartial commentator, although I've done it myself quite a few times. Are you sitting comfortably? Then we'll begin.

Hello. I'm Chris Foote Wood. According to my reckoning, this is my nineteenth book. I haven't written it for money - whatever profit/royalties I make will go to one or more of Vic's charities - but for the record. More of that later. Let's start at the beginning. I was born Christopher Wood on the 15th December 1940 at Collar House, Prestbury, the first child and only son of Stanley and Helen (Nellie) Wood. Later there were three daughters, Penelope (born 1945), Rosalind (1950) and Victoria (1953), so there were thirteen years between me and my famous and hugely talented youngest sister.

Collar House was taken over as a maternity hospital in WW2. I often wonder if being born in a stately home deep in the Cheshire countryside had an effect on baby Christopher (oops, there I go again, third person. Stop it!) I fondly imagine myself as a baby, spending much of the first nine days of my life in a cot on the veranda overlooking perfect lawns and clipped hedges, thinking 'I've cracked it, born into the aristocracy!' Then to be taken away with Mum to rented rooms in Cheadle Hulme, what a let-down!

But my childhood was incredibly happy. I felt so secure with Mum and Dad (even though they were often out working), Nana and Grandad (Stan's parents) and Granny Mape (Mum's Mum, her Dad died soon after I was born) all caring for me. The last twelve months of WW2 and the year after, I lived with my Dad's parents in Manchester. M&D stayed in Plymouth (Stan was in the Royal Navy) where my first sister Penelope was born.

I was the first grandchild, my father an only child, so Nana and Grandad 'spoiled me rotten'. From the age of three and a half, they would have me perform on a little stool next to the upright piano (with candelabra) in the rarely-used front parlour. I had to sing, recite or play a musical instrument. The point was, no matter how bad my performance was, it was received with wild applause. I've been seeking wild applause ever since!

After short spells at infant schools in Plymouth and Manchester, I fetched up at Alderman Smith's Infants in Bury and then the nearby St Stephen's C of E juniors before getting a scholarship to Bury Grammar Boys, an independent fee-paying day school. There was only one Kay scholarship on offer each year, and I got it! I had plenty of brain power (thank you, Mum and Dad) but lacked practical skills. As my wife Frances used to say, 'how come you are so clever but have no common sense?'

So I was normally top of the class and sailed through my GCE 'O' levels and 'A' levels, winning scholarships to Manchester and Durham universities. Not wanting to live at home, I chose Durham, a four-year BSc honours degree course in civil engineering at King's College, Newcastle. Exempt the first year, I passed all my maths finals at the end of year 2 and passed all the year 2 and year 3 exams and took my remaining Finals to complete the course. I was not awarded a degree and was refused leave to re-sit my Finals. For this I must thank Prof Fisher Cassie, head of the CEng department. He did me an enormous favour: if he had given me a degree (for him, it was 'honours or nothing') I would never have met my loving wife and life partner Frances.

My first wife Helena Emilia Pietruszka and I were both students at King's when we married in 1961. Refused the consent of her parents, we eloped to Scotland: not to Gretna Green (not much to do there) but to Edinburgh for the Festival! We had a great time (both virgins, we stayed in separate boarding houses) for the two-week qualifying period and married a week later on a Saturday day trip to the Scottish capital.

Helena and I had three children but divorced in 1976 after fifteen years of marriage. H told me in 1971 or early 1972 that she wanted a divorce: at that stage I would have preferred to have stayed married to H, but said I wouldn't stand in her way. I then met Frances (from Mitcham, South London) at the Open University in August 1972. Next year she came to be with me in Bishop Auckland, and we married in 1977. We had no children. Frances died of cancer in 2013 after forty years together. For the last few months of her life, I was her carer.

From an early age I was writing letters to my Nana and Grandad: aged eight, I produced a handwritten 'newspaper', the *Wood News*. Headline: 'the chip butty question'. My upwardly mobile parents had banned chip butties, one of my favourite foods. Unable to confront them directly, I made my plea in print. Aged ten, I had a poem published in the *News Chronicle*. Aged fifteen, I had eight or nine girl pen-friends of a similar age all around the UK, writing letters of thirteen pages or more to all of them. One year I hitch-hiked all around the country and snogged most of these really nice girls.

My Dad Stan was a writer, and a very good one. He could and should have been famous, but 'never gave up the day job' (insurance). He encouraged me to write, and predicted I would be a famous novelist. (Sorry, Dad, unlike you and Vic, I'm no good at fiction). A freelance journalist in his younger days, Dad impressed on me to 'always have more than one string to your bow'. At sixteen, I was writing the weekly athletics column for the *Bury Times*. I wrote for the college newspaper *Courier* and edited the student arts magazine *Northerner*. It was the only time *Northerner* made a profit.

After leaving uni I became a part-time sports correspondent for various local newspapers. My 'day job' was in civil engineering, and in 1964 I became senior assistant engineer with Bishop Auckland UDC. Next I was bridge and section engineer, helping build the A1(M) motorway through County Durham. Words were still my passion, and in 1968 I made journalism my main occupation. I claim to have been the first in the UK to publish commercial free press newspapers. Starting with the Auckland Advertiser, I built up a stable of six community newspapers with my first company Durham Free Press. Rivals quickly appeared on the scene. Unable to compete with all-advertising sheets (my newspapers were 50/50 editorial/advertising) I gave it up and returned to civil engineering, helping build a new ten-mile section of the A19 trunk road across Teesside.

But the writing bug was too strong, and I again became a full-time journo, setting up and running my own regional press agency North Press News & Sport. This ran for thirty years, 1974 to 2004 when I sold it off to concentrate on writing and publishing books as author/editor/publisher. Some of my books have been produced by other publishers, but most have been self-published under my own imprint, Northern Writers. As well as my own books, I have edited and/or published books by other authors.

In 2007 I fulfilled a lifetime ambition and went around every British seaside pleasure pier (fifty-six in all). The following year I repeated the feat to promote my book *Walking Over the Waves - Quintessential British Seaside Piers.* In my traditional pier garb of straw boater, stripy blazer etc, I led the 'Great British Pier Crawl' and did a mini *End of the Pier* show on many of 'em.

My piers book and *Nellie's Book* are the most popular subjects for the Author Talks I give to WIs and other organisations in the North East and Yorkshire, charging modest expenses only. I also give talks on Charles Dickens and 'how to be a writer'. My biggest audience was 500 for my public lecture on disgraced local politician T Dan Smith, based on my controversial biography of a man I greatly admired but had feet of clay. Former Newcastle City Council Leader TDS was jailed for six years for corruption in the 1970s, but in my book I argue he was not guilty of the crime for which he was convicted.

In the early 1970s, much of my income came from freelancing with local radio stations like Radio Tees, Metro Radio and Radio Newcastle, reporting news and sport. It was a great experience: I got to interview some top sports stars and leading politicians. It's my proud boast that I worked for Radio Durham at the same time as Kate Adie who I much admire. Hasn't she done well?

As a boy, I was into everything. I joined the Cubs and the Scouts and enjoyed every minute: camping, hiking, trekking, indoor and outdoor games. At school there was the Choir and clubs for Stamps, Railways and Chess: I was in them all, the YMCA and the local athletics club. I took part in school plays and music competitions, and competed for BGS in athletics and cross-country. This latter activity only started at sixteen: for three years I had not been allowed anything strenuous due to contracting TB on my lungs. For three months I had to lie still in bed at home, tended by my very cross Mother who did her duty with undisguised ill grace.

Thanks to M&D's anti-church views, none of us four children was baptised, almost unheard of in those days. At fourteen, I had a religious conversion and got myself baptised in Bury's main C of E church, St Mary's. I sang with the Tenterden Street Baptist Youth Choir and at sixteen was secretary of two church youth clubs, C of E and Baptist. I was a member of Bury Youth Council and after one of my speeches an old gadgie said to me 'you should be an MP, son'. Sad to say, I didn't make it. And my adherence to the church ended after six years of intense involvement as an evangelist, preaching on street corners and in Newcastle's Bigg Market on a Sunday evening. I still adhere to Christian values and sing in a local Methodist choir, but I do not belong to any church.

As well as writing, Dad encouraged me to take an interest in politics. After WW2, Stan was Liberal agent for the constituency of Bury and Radcliffe. He was canny enough to insure the deposit in the 1950 general election, a disaster for the Liberal Party with over 400 deposits lost. Aged nine, I was Dad's 'gofer' at that election, and learned all about politics and election organisation. Most importantly, as soon as I could read he told me to read the *News Chronicle* every day, so from the age of six I was well up on national and international affairs.

Aged sixteen, I joined the Young Liberals and became their national Vice-Chair and Chair of the Northern region YLs. At uni I was first secretary and then Chair of the Liberal Society, and was also elected press officer of the National Union of Liberal Students. I wrote for and helped publish the NULS magazine *Radical*. From 1963 to 2015 I was a local and national candidate for the Liberals/Liberal Democrats forty-two times, fighting eight Westminster and six European elections, all in the North East, plus once for elected Mayor of Middlesbrough (2011). Needless to say I was not elected as MP, MEP or Mayor.

But I was a local councillor in Bishop Auckland for forty years, quite some feat in a Labour stronghold. I was also a Durham county councillor for twelve years and a Dene Valley parish councillor for seven years, inaugural Chair when the parish council was formed in 2000. I was also Chair of Wear Valley Council 1976-77 and Council Leader for six years, 1976-79 and 1991-94. I was the first LibDem to represent the North East on the EU Council of the Regions, 2005-07.

Somehow I found time to do the heavy lifting as a party official. Since re-forming the Bishop Auckland constituency party in 1972, I was Chair and/or secretary of both the constituency and town parties for over thirty years, recruiting and training members and candidates, organising elections and raising the money to pay for them. I wrote most of our election leaflets and arranged their distribution: all this with only a handful of members, with Frances always to the fore.

For over thirty years I was an active regional party officer, including eighteen years as Regional President and twelve years as Vice-Chairman. With my wife as Regional Secretary for twenty years, I never stood as Regional Chair to avoid too much power in one household. All very boring stuff, but I was happy to do it. Without dedicated volunteers like me and Frances, there would be no democracy.

Being married to two teachers (but not at the same time!) I got to know something about education and was a school governor for thirty-five years, Chair of Governors for most of that time. As a councillor I found myself on numerous local bodies, helping set up two community associations and playing an active part in their development. When I stood down as a councillor in 2007, I was made an Honorary Alderman of both Wear Valley and Durham County. An Honorary Alderman twice over, you bet I'm proud!

Somehow, I found time to be secretary of Bishop Auckland Athletic Club and the town's Debating Society, also running folk nights, fashion shows, youth sports, training a junior soccer team, driving a community mini-bus, calling bingo numbers - not all at the same time, I hasten to add. I was press officer of Bishop Auckland football, cricket and rugby clubs and also reported on swimming, water polo and numerous other sports. My sports editor at Radio Tees was Jeff Stelling, now a national TV presenter.

After running for the school (bronze medal in the Northern Schools mile) and Durham University, I gave up athletics at twenty when I got married. Inspired by my hero Chris Brasher and his fantastic description in *The Observer* of running in the New York marathon, at forty I became a 'born again' runner. In 1981 I ran the first London marathon (interviewing Brasher for the *Evening Gazette* afterwards) and the first Great North Run (half marathon). In all I ran thirteen full marathons and many more half marathons, including the first twenty-five GNRs, plus numerous other road and track races from 100 metres to 10k, plus the occasional cross-country event.

Later I took up the triathlon (swim, bike, run) and did mini- and full Olympic tris including the London Triathlon. I raced on my bike in 10, 25 and 50-mile time trials, I did road racing and raced on the track at Croft motor-racing circuit. Forced to stop running at seventy due to wear and tear on the knees, I now keep fit by walking, cycling, swimming and gym. I'm proud to have competed in the British, European and World Masters (veterans) athletic championships. I have won a few age group trophies at local level. The last race I won was the over-70s 3,000 metres in the North East Veterans athletic championships at Jarrow in 2011 just before my compulsory (and much regretted) retirement from the sport.

As well as entertaining the grandparents, from an early age I was regularly in pantomime. It's my boast that I have played every part in panto except principal boy! In 2015 I returned to panto as the Beast in *Beauty and the Beast* at the Northallerton Forum. I was also with the Bishop Auckland Little Theatre for many years, almost always cast as a 'heavy', a villain or a detective.

My early piano lessons stood me in good stead when I caught the rock and roll bug in 1955. I taught myself to play the ukulele, banjo and guitar, although my first instrument was a washboard in a Bury skiffle group. My parents, well-off by that time, were supposed to 'top up' my uni grant of £65 a year. They paid my term-time Hall fees but did not provide any cash, so I had to earn my money from music, especially when I was 'barred out' of the family home and had to fend for myself during uni vacations.

I had a rock group, the Deltics, which went as far as making a demo disc but no further. I had a seven-piece dance band, the Collegians, and played for fun in a trad jazz band and a much bigger jazz orchestra. I did a few gigs as a solo folk singer, but my main income came from promoting. As well as running the 61 Club for three years, three nights a week (Friday folk, Saturday rock, Sunday jazz), I organised pop/rock concerts at various North East venues, booking the bands, printing the tickets and posters and arranging security. I was tough: any group that turned up late didn't get paid.

I had always wanted to do a one-man show, and finally got round to it with *The Genius of Charles Dickens* with which I made my professional stage debut at Chorley in 2013, aged seventy-two. My twenty year-old granddaughter Emily Wood made her debut at the Edinburgh Festival Fringe that year, and I followed her a year later making my debut with my *Dickens* show. There are over 3,000 shows at the Fringe, but we managed to fill a small venue. Thus encouraged, I returned to Edinburgh with some success with the same show in 2015 and 2016.

When Frances died in 2013, I decided to do as much variety of work as possible. As well as writing and performing, I am now a professional lecturer with Nadfas, the National Association of Decorative Fine Arts Societies, having passed their very stringent tests. Thus far I have been asked to give lectures on Seaside Piers and Dickens, including two dates on the Isle of Man on consecutive days.

After receiving excellent training with the Fellowship of Independent Celebrants, I now write and conduct non-religious weddings and funerals. Non-religious ceremonies can and should be just as serious, meaningful and joyful as any church or register office ceremony. Fewer and fewer people attend church, and with ceremonies able to take place almost anywhere, more and more people are opting for something different. I pride myself in writing and conducting a service unique to the couple marrying or to the person who has died. So far, this part of my work, which I took up only this year (2016), has been enormously satisfying and greatly appreciated.

It has been a huge privilege to have such a fantastically talented sister as Victoria. I have had the great joy of following her career from its earliest beginnings. I most admire the single-minded determination she showed in making her very individual brand of humour such a huge success, as well as her writing and dramatic performances. Then there was producing and directing, again with great success. I am in awe of Vic's huge talent, which greatly overshadows my own modest abilities.

Another factor I admire is her innate business sense. After many mistakes early in her career, Vic became adept at making the most of her opportunities with books, CDs and videos to add to her successful tours and TV shows. Much of her work was channelled through her own company. Undoubtedly a multi-millionaire (and deservedly so), Vic never wasted money or indulged in expensive whims. A hugely successful showbiz star living in London's very posh Highgate, Lancashire lass Vic never became a 'luvvie' and made sure her children did not grow up as 'showbiz' kids.

For me, this book has been a labour of love. Any money I make from it will go to one or more of Vic's favourite charities. I wish I had had more time to go more deeply into the full extent of Vic's work, but time was short. It was always planned for this book to come out in time for Christmas 2016, but I was messed about by one well-known national publisher who withdrew after I had signed the contract they had sent me! And that was after several weeks of negotiations.

When other national publishers also expressed their reservations, I turned to a local publisher and an old friend, Lynn Davidson of The Memoir Club. Based in Washington in the North East, Lynn is a vastly experienced editor and publisher. I will be forever grateful for her hard work, her positive approach and her determination to make this book a success.

Chris Foote Wood
Darlington
November 2016